Acclaim for
FAMILIES *of* VALUE

"Robert Bernstein's book, *Families of Value,* is a brilliant and persuasive response to those religious conservatives who extol 'family values,' while oppressing homosexual people. He confronts the irrational prejudice against same-sex parents with consciousness raising, real life stories. This book will open hearts and minds and move this debate to a whole new place. That is a major accomplishment."
—**John Shelby Spong,** Bishop, author of *The Sins of Scripture: Exposing the Bible's Texts of Hate to Discover the God of Love*

"One of the most flagrantly dishonest arguments being made in American politics today comes from those who seek to cloak their dislike of gay men and lesbians behind purported concern for children. In fact, opposition to same-sex marriage means, where children are concerned, that young people with gay or lesbian parents are victimized emotionally and legally, not by the gay men and lesbians who love them, but by those who put obstacles in the way of that love. The compelling, documented stories in this book make clear that allowing same-sex marriage is in fact a strongly pro-child policy."
—**The Honorable Barney Frank (D-MA)**

"This book tells stories of real people who are demonstrating courage and love to raise children as gay parents. Robert's first book, *Straight Parents, Gay Children,* is only exceeded by the moving stories in this book. If you read this book you will learn a lot about the love and dedication these parents are devoting to raising healthy and well adjusted children."
—**The Honorable Richard Gephardt,** former Majority Leader and Democratic Leader of the House of Representatives

"Bernstein's book lets couples and their kids tell their own moving stories, bringing us to the heart of the debate over gay people's freedom to marry. Their poignant accounts show what every study tells—gay parents are at least as fit as non-gay parents, and their children are at least as emotionally sound and well-adjusted even while, against all logic, the law punishes these kids by depriving them of the safety-net and security that marriage would bring."

—**Evan Wolfson,** Executive Director of Freedom to Marry, author of *Why Marriage Matters,* named by *Time* magazine as one of the "100 Most Influential People in the World"

"Through the sensitive description of real-life examples, Robert A. Bernstein profoundly spells out one of the most complex issues of our time, the rights of same-sex couples and their children to support, protection, and inclusion within our communities. His book portrays the value, health and loving care in these families, achieved through all kinds of negativity."

—**Edmond L.** Browning, XXIV Presiding Bishop, Episcopal Church

About the Author

ROBERT A. BERNSTEIN, MA, JD, has served as a supervisory trial attorney for the U.S. Department of Justice and as associate professor of law at Southern Methodist University School of Law. From 1988 to 1995 he was national vice president of PFLAG (Parents, Families and Friends of Lesbians and Gays). As a freelance writer, his writing has appeared in more than sixty daily newspapers, including the *New York Times, Chicago Tribune*, and the *Washington Post*, as well as many gay publications. In 1996 he was named "Parent of the Week" by the Oprah Winfrey Show. His previous book, *Straight Parents, Gay Children: Keeping Families Together*, won the Award for Best Scholarship on the Subject of Intolerance by the Gustavus Myers Center for the Study of Human Rights in North America. He and his wife divide their time between Bethesda, Maryland and Portland, Oregon.

FAMILIES

of

VALUE

Also by Robert A. Bernstein

Straight Parents, Gay Children

FAMILIES

of

VALUE

**Personal Profiles of Pioneering
Lesbian and Gay Parents**

Robert A. Bernstein

MARLOWE & COMPANY
NEW YORK

FAMILIES OF VALUE:
Personal Profiles of Pioneering Lesbian and Gay Parents
Copyright © 2005 by Robert A. Bernstein

Published by
Marlowe & Company
An Imprint of Avalon Publishing Group Incorporated
245 West 17th Street • 11th Floor
New York, NY 10011-5300

Grateful acknowledgment is made to COLAGE (Children of Lesbians and Gays Everywhere), for permission to reprint *Focus on My Family: A Queerspawn Anthology* in Chapter 5.

Library of Congress Cataloging-in-Publication Data

Bernstein, Robert, 1926–
    Families of value : personal profiles of pioneering lesbian and gay parents /
    Robert A. Bernstein.
       p. cm.
    ISBN 1-56025-638-9 (pbk.)

      1. Gay parents—United States. 2. Lesbian mothers—United States.
      3. Gay fathers—United States. I. Title.

HQ75.28.U6B47 2005
306.874'086'640973—dc22

2005003744

9 8 7 6 5 4 3 2 1

Designed by Maria Elias

Printed in Canada

*To the millions of children worldwide who daily have to
deal with the fallout from the unwarranted cultural
stigma against their gay and lesbian parents*

CONTENTS

Introduction

N early two decades ago, my younger daughter acknowledged to herself and to her family that she was a lesbian. I wasn't surprised by the disclosure itself. I had long considered the possibility she was gay—even, as I would learn, while she herself was still undergoing a painful period of denial. I *was* surprised, however, by the enriching experience the disclosure touched off for me personally.

In the ensuing months and years, I met scores of fine people who happened to be lesbian, gay, bisexual, or transgendered. I came to profoundly admire the courage and integrity of the pioneers among them who were openly braving the forces of ignorance while leading society to a deeper understanding of human diversity. And I took inspiration, too, from many of their parents, who often put their own lives and careers on the line in defense of their children's right—and spiritual need—to live free of deception. I was moved to write my first book, *Straight Parents, Gay Children: Keeping Families Together* (Thunder's Mouth Press, second edition, 2003).

My lesbian daughter and her partner of sixteen years have so far not seen fit to have children. (They left it to my heterosexual daughter and her husband to confer grandparenthood upon me.) Meanwhile, however, other lesbians and gay men are parenting a new generation of Americans. And I find myself once more inspired by a pioneer cadre who refuse to allow cultural bias to derail their inner-directed destiny.

So it is that I have written here another book about the ultimate triumph of courage and integrity. It is the story of some of the pioneer families who are inevitably moving same-sex parenting into the national mainstream.

Like it or not—and granted that most Americans still do not—millions of children are already being raised by gay and lesbian parents, and their numbers are increasing at an ever-accelerating pace. Definitive statistics are still hard to come by, and estimates of their numbers run an extensive gamut from one to fourteen million. (For example, the National Adoption Information Clearinghouse has placed the figure at somewhere between six and fourteen million, the Human Rights

Campaign at one to nine million.) In all likelihood, the lower estimate of one million is probably closest to the mark, according to Stanford Law Professor Michael Wald, a family law specialist who conducted an extensive study of families headed by same-sex parents. But whatever the number, it is already sizable, and the crest of an irresistible wave of the future. Meanwhile, however, it is the children who suffer most from the hostility spawned by residual bias.

Cultural attitudes are changing rapidly. Just a few years ago, lesbians and gay men were societal pariahs. Now, while the issue of gay marriage per se stirs a deep cultural divide, opposition to legal recognition of gay civil unions, conferring many of the legal incidents of marriage, has declined sharply. And every reliable poll indicates that younger people are far more apt than their elders to support full equal rights for gay and lesbian couples.

Those who continue to resist the tide typically phrase their opposition in religious terms. But the true divide is in fact probably not religious but generational.

One stunning example is a February 2004 Baylor University student newspaper editorial strongly endorsing gay marriage. Baylor, located in Waco, Texas, bills itself as the largest Baptist university in the world—a bastion of Christian fundamentalism in the heart of perhaps the most conservative state in the Union. So, predictably, the editorial was instantly denounced by university officials.

But the fact remains that on this issue these young Christians, however otherwise devoted to their conservative religion, found themselves 180 degrees apart from their church elders. "Gay couples should be granted the same equal rights to legal marriage as heterosexual couples," they wrote. They acknowledged that "many gay couples share deep bonds of love" and should "be allowed to enjoy the benefits and happiness of marriage." They likened discrimination based on sexual orientation to that based on color, ethnicity or religious beliefs.

Back in 2001, about 70 percent of American high school seniors supported gay marriage, according to a poll conducted by researchers at Hamilton College in Clinton, New York, with the assistance of the polling firm Zogby International. This compared to an approval rate of about a third among older Americans in a Gallup poll.

The message for opponents of same-sex unions is clear. They are fighting a doomed, rearguard action. They are fighting millions of loving, dedicated, courageous, family-centered parents and children who will not be denied respect.

The ultimate outcome of the fight seems certain. What is not clear is how long it will last.

Or how many innocent children it will wound in the process.

The families portrayed here are not typical or representative of those headed by same-sex parents. They have been leaders in bringing about the social change that is gradually easing the way to their acceptance. Most of them live in communities—often due in significant part to their own efforts—that have by now largely adjusted to the reality of their presence. By personal temperament, they combine qualities of caring and sensitivity with those of courage, candor, and dedication. So chance has supplied them with both the demography and the emotional mettle to serve as pioneers. For millions of others who lack some of the same inherent advantages, by chance of geographical location and/or other personal circumstances, the path obviously can be far more difficult.

But even the hardiest of pioneers have found the way clogged with underbrush and land mines. Among those you'll meet here are the following:

- A lesbian couple who deliberately placed themselves and their children in the eye of a campaign firestorm of antigay animosity and violence—to the ultimate benefit of the entire family.

- A gay father of two, a theologically conservative Protestant minister, who choked up in a Sunday sermon, bringing tears to the eyes of his mostly heterosexual congregation, as he described the animosity of legislators to whom he had tried to explain the dangers posed to his sons by a proposed antigay law.

- A gay couple acclaimed and honored as outstanding foster parents of five children born with AIDS—but who have been nonetheless forced to defend against a state's attempt to strip one of their children, now a happy, healthy, well-adjusted teenager, from the only family he's ever known.

- Two lesbian police officers, concerned about their daughters in the event one of the mothers were killed in the line of duty, who waged a public campaign for the extension of police death benefits to same-sex couples.

- A lesbian lawyer who utilized her position as a city attorney to further the local climate of acceptance for her children.

- Gay dads whose nurturing instinct drove them to brave the frontiers of gay male parenting.

I think you'll find their stories as moving as I have.

More disturbing than the ultimately doomed rush to outlaw gay marriage is the usual rationale set forth in support of such a ban, namely, the need to "protect children." It's an argument that is profoundly and tragically ironic. It is not merely wrong—but itself generates untold harm to children.

How are millions (and counting) of innocent children protected when they hear politicians and religious leaders denounce their parents as deviants who are out to corrupt them? When the Vatican, seat of the most powerful church in the world, tells them that their parents are "doing violence" to them? When they read that they are destined to become social and psychological misfits? When they lack adequate health care because they are not covered by the insurance policy of a parent's life partner? When they face poverty because a parent is ineligible for the survivor benefits of his or her partner? When they are denied lifesaving treatment because a hospital emergency room refuses to recognize the authority of a parent's partner?

And more prosaically, but no less profoundly, how are children protected when daily, at school and elsewhere, they are stigmatized, harassed, and discriminated against because their parents happen to be part of an unjustly disfavored minority?

Small wonder, then, that virtually every leading professional organization involved with child welfare has issued statements supporting the rights of gay parents and their children. Among others, those organizations include the American Academy of Pediatrics, the American Psychological Association, the National Association of Social Workers, the American Psychiatric Association, the American Medical Association, the American Academy of Family Physicians, the American Association of Child and Adolescent Psychiatrists, the American Psychoanalytic Association, and the American Bar Association. (See Appendix A for many of these groups' policy statements and positions.)

There is, of course, no reason why families with gay and lesbian parents should escape the problems that plague all families. They are hardly immune, for example, from the scourges of poverty, addiction, child abuse, depression, truancy, or adolescent rebellion. But are there additional, undue risks for children of lesbians and gay men? Or are their particular risks, those special to families with same-sex parents, simply those that arise from cultural bias?

To that latter question, every reliable sociological study responds with a resounding "Yea."

Dr. Judith Stacey is a New York University sociologist who is generally recognized as the nation's foremost expert on studies of children of same-sex parents. She and another sociologist conducted an intensive review of studies on the subject and concluded that such parents "are as fit, effective and successful as heterosexual parents" and that their children "are as emotionally healthy and socially adjusted and at least as educational and socially successful as children raised by heterosexual parents."

Far from putting their children at additional risk, reason strongly suggests that the average gay and lesbian couple are apt to be *more* prepared and *more* devoted parents than their average heterosexual counterpart. There are no accidental same-sex parents. Nor do they have children simply because it is what is expected of them by their own parents, their peers or their culture. They have children, rather, by choice—because they are impelled by a nurturing instinct sufficiently strong that they're willing to take on formidable cultural barriers to do so.

Dr. Judith Stacey's view on this point is instructive:

"There are lots of reasons to think that on average gay and lesbian parents—and to some extent gay dads in particular—are better parents for a whole host of reasons that social scientists call selection factors. They tend to be older and better educated. They obviously really, really, really want to be parents. And they have to overcome a lot of things to get to that point.

"So you're already eliminating a whole host of heterosexual parents who just sort of bumble into it, or do it at any imaginable age."

This is the story of some brave families who did not "bumble into it."

FAMILIES

of

VALUE

I.

Finding Ways to Make Change

At age twelve, Alex Tinker turned a major corner
of his life. It grew out of an incident that led to
the only school suspension of a boy raised by a devoutly
Quaker mother and headed for academic and athletic
laurels.

It happened because a classmate capped an argument
between them by snarling, "Your mother is a lezzie."

The taunt was nothing new. Reared by lesbian parents,
Alex, though heterosexual, had himself been called
"fairy" and "sissy boy" as well as hearing his mother
referred to as "a lezzie," "fag," or "dyke." But until that

moment, he says he had "tried to keep a low profile" and refused to respond outwardly to the provocations.

This time was different. As Alex would tell his birth mother, "You're the pacifist here. I'm not a pacifist and I just decided I wasn't going to take it any more." Years later, as a high school senior being interviewed by Barbara Walters on ABC's *20/20*, he would explain his reaction in rather more graphic terms:

"I went off on him and just beat the crap out of him, basically."

Both boys were suspended. But for Alex, it was nevertheless a positive experience in the life of a youth who in high school would be a National Honor Society scholar, a varsity track runner, and a participant in a prestigious Johns Hopkins University program for talented youth.

Now in his fourth year at the University of Oregon with a double major in political science and economics, Alex recalls how the fight and suspension changed his attitude about dealing with the reality of his unconventional family.

"It was out in the open, and I stopped trying to hide it. And from then on, I didn't get any more flack about it either. I wasn't ashamed or embarrassed about it anymore.

"If you're open and comfortable with it, it doesn't leave room for anyone to taunt you about it."

Alex is the youngest of three children who grew up in a household headed by his biological mother Bonnie Tinker and her mate Sara Graham. For him, that spawned a range of emotions: resentment, guilt, shame, blame, anger—but also love and respect for his mothers, who he told Walters are "as in love and committed to each other as any straight married couple."

And in the end, whatever the unpleasantness en route, Alex now says, "I wouldn't have had it any other way. The experience made me a stronger person."

Alex is twelve years younger than his sister Connie, and sixteen years younger than his big brother Josh. So it was his good fortune to be the beneficiary of motherly wisdom painfully acquired over the years, and derived in part from his siblings' earlier travails. The mothers had learned of the dangers, and ultimate futility, of the closet as a means of "protecting" their children. They had discovered that societal stigma could be even more devastating to the children than to themselves. (When just twelve years old, Alex interpreted the invective of antigay leaders as in effect calling him "a bastard" and telling him he "shouldn't have been born.") And they had concluded that openness and activism were the family's most potent tools against cultural ignorance.

For the women, one important insight came when Alex was five and suffered his first deeply hurtful blow as the child of same-sex parents. Bonnie's voice still catches as she tells the story.

Alex and a little neighbor girl, Nicole, had been inseparable best friends between his toddler and kindergarten years. When they were about four, they asked Bonnie where babies came from, and Alex was disappointed to learn that as a boy he wouldn't be able to have a baby himself. Bonnie told him not to worry, that he probably would one day fall in love with a woman who could have a baby for both of them.

"Alex said, 'Oh, how will I ever find anyone to marry me? And Nicole, sitting next to him, put her arms around him and said, 'Oh, Alex, I'll marry you.'"

Bonnie sighs, "The kids were that tight."

So it came as a terrible shock about a year later when Nicole's father prohibited her from continuing see Alex. He did it out of religious beliefs because Bonnie and Sara were lesbians. Bonnie says it was "like a death for all of us," but with "no support groups for mourning the loss."

Alex was so disturbed that Bonnie and Sara took him to a counselor. "I felt we had essentially a suicidal kindergartner," Bonnie says.

"The fact was that I had brought this child into a world where he was going to face hate, and it was going to hurt him. From that moment, it was perfectly clear to me that my life had to be completely dedicated to changing that world. And to helping my children learn that when they were faced with injustice of any sort, the way to respond was to find ways to make change."

Bonnie herself became commercial radio's first host of a morning rush hour talk show devoted to gay and lesbian issues. She is also the founder of Love Makes A Family, a leading advocacy organization to which Sara and their three children have all devoted countless hours. And their activism would in turn cast Alex into the midst of statewide cultural warfare that descended on Oregon when he was still just eight.

Their family story hit an emotional high point on April 17, 2004, when Bonnie and Sara were married, in Quaker terminology, "under the care" of the Multnomah

Friends Meeting and with the official, if still legally ambiguous, blessing of a county marriage license. The ceremony was held at a private club because the Friends' Meeting House was too small to handle a crowd of 250 that included some fifty members of the Meeting, the couple's three children; their only surviving parent, Bonnie's mother Lorena Jeanne; and a bevy of brothers, sisters, cousins, nieces and nephews from as far away as Michigan, Missouri, and Massachusetts. Sara's cousin, a Catholic nun and music teacher, closed the formal ceremony with a piano rendition of Beethoven's "Moonlight Sonata."

One guest was a United States congressman—Dennis Kucinich, the only presidential candidate of that year who supported gay marriage. The congressman's website on the following day displayed a picture of Kucinich with the two brides, plus a close-up inset of the women cutting their wedding cake—appropriately topped by tiny figurines of two white-gowned brides.

Despite the celebratory hullabaloo, and the decorative marriage certificate framed on their living room wall, their union, like that of some 3,000 other same-sex Oregon weddings in March and April of 2004, still remained in legal limbo pending review by the state's voters and Supreme Court. (see chapters 4 and 9.) But the legal question mark failed to stem the traditional tears that flowed from the eyes of wedding guests who had watched the Tinker-Graham family struggle through the years toward that symbolic spiritual moment.

Bonnie and Sara lament that social change came too late to save Josh from a difficult childhood and a disastrous

first marriage to a fervidly antigay woman. They have
no regret whatever, on the other hand, for the fact that
their middle child, Connie, turned out to be gay herself
—even though in a homophobic culture that's what
many same-sex parents most dread. (One lesbian
mother, fighting in an often hostile court system for custody of her two children from an earlier marriage,
reportedly told Dan Cherubin, a high-profile gay son of
gay parents: "Nothing personal, Dan, but you're my
worst nightmare.") And their pride in all of their children is ever transparent.

At first glance, the family heritage of both Bonnie and
Sara would appear so conventionally mainstream as to
belie their nonconformist adult paths.

Bonnie's father Leonard Tinker was a Methodist minister, the son of a small-town upstate New York shop-
keeper. He and her mother Lorena Jeanne, a native
Texan, met at Northwestern University when he was a
seminary student and she was earning a master's degree
in religious education. Bonnie is one of six children born
while their father served a series of small town Iowa
churches and one in Des Moines. Bonnie remembers
him as a "born preacher" with "great oral style," as well
as an accomplished fiddler and square dancer. Her
mother was outwardly a prototypical minister's wife,
maintaining a spotless house twenty-four hours seven
days a week, because as Bonnie puts it: "Church people
could and did drop in at any time of the day, and they

could and did report to everyone else on the condition of the parsonage."

Sara was the fourth child and only daughter of a Portland Irish Catholic family, born ten years after the youngest of her three brothers. Her father was a lifelong member of the carpenter's union and an outspoken Democrat, the son of an even more outspoken Socialist. Her mother, of mixed Irish and French Canadian stock, worked as a secretary until Sara's birth and was later active in parish work. Two of her brothers became police officers; the other spent two years in seminary before leaving to go into business. Several of her cousins became nuns, one of whom was a hospital administrator and another president of Portland's Marylhurst College (now Marylhurst University).

So both Bonnie and Sara can point to garden-variety Middle American roots. But a closer look at their early years reveals some of the seeds of the crusading passion that would ultimately shape the lives of their own convention-defying family.

Leonard Tinker's small-town ministries, for example, turn out to have sparked a series of civil rights confrontations, the last of them triggered by his crusade to integrate the Atlantic, Iowa, town swimming pool. Bonnie, then in second grade, says she "didn't know exactly what was going on but I gradually got the feeling that nobody liked me."

In the end, very few liked her father, either, and at the congregants' insistence, the Bishop moved him to a Des Moines church. There, however, he continued his civil rights work, and when he became active in opposing the

Vietnam War, he had once again overstepped church limits. Faced with the prospect of being exiled once more to a small-town church, where the pay would be inadequate to support his growing family, he signed on as an administrator with the American Friends Service Committee, an international organization that works for peace and justice on principles of nonviolence. There, he was able to spend his days, until his death in 1978, working full-time for social justice issues without fear of job reprisal.

Nor, despite the burdens of raising six children while maintaining a spick-and-span parsonage, did Bonnie's mother Lorena Jeanne fit the stereotype of primly proper minister's wife. She was as devoted as her husband to civil rights causes, and ultimately became a well-known activist in her own right.

Unlike Bonnie's, Sara's family engaged in no overt social or civil rights activism. But her parents nevertheless somehow instilled in her—perhaps simply by their kindness and social justice concerns—a profound hate of prejudice. She recalls that even as a very young child, she always reacted strongly against any hint of discriminatory bias. And she feels that her Catholic schools probably helped nurture her evolving passion for social fairness, thanks to the Gospel teachings of equality, love and justice.

There can be no doubt, in any event, that Sara's ingrained passion against prejudice factored importantly in her first major flaunting of mainstream norms. At the age of nineteen, while a student at Portland State University, she fell in love with John Graham—a handsome young African American.

However fair-minded Sara's parents might have been at heart, they were simply not culturally prepared in the mid-'60s to welcome a Negro, as blacks were then known, into the family. Appalled, they insisted that Sara transfer from Portland State, located in downtown Portland, to a residence hall at Marylhurst College some nine miles outside the city and then operated by the Sisters of the Holy Names of Jesus and Mary. Her family might as well have spared themselves the trouble. Sara quickly found a path through the thick woods abutting the campus to reach River Road, where John would pick her up to drive into town. After one semester, they allowed her to return to Portland State, but once they realized she was still seeing John, they renewed their strenuous efforts to end the affair.

Her middle brother—who would ultimately welcome John into the family, and who years later would be among those present at her marriage to Bonnie—even threatened in one fit of anger to kill John. And that did register with Sara, who decided she'd better get out of town altogether. But after a few years in San Francisco and New York, never out of touch with John, she returned to Portland. Before long, she became pregnant with Josh; John and Sara were married shortly before his birth.

The birth of Josh softened the family's aversion. Both John and Sara returned to school and Sara had completed a degree in psychology at Portland State when John died suddenly of a heart attack. Josh was just five and a half years old.

Sara earned a master's degree in counseling at another Portland university, Lewis and Clark, and worked as a counselor and social justice advocate for women victims of drugs, poverty, and the criminal justice system.

A few years later, she came to the awareness that she was a lesbian. And shortly thereafter, in 1975, she took a job as counselor at a home for battered women, the Bradley-Angle House. There, she fell in love with the home's founding director, Bonnie Tinker, whose zigzag course to Portland had been by way of two years of study under some internationally-known, mostly radical, thinkers in Cuernavaca, Mexico.

There, a conference on women's issues in Latin America, at which Bonnie served as translator, would chart the course for the remainder of her life.

Until then, she had never given a thought to the matter of sexual orientation. But some of the thirty women at the seminar wanted to talk about lesbianism. Bonnie recalls: "I had no idea why we should talk about lesbianism. I was from Iowa. My dad was a Methodist preacher. I didn't know lesbians existed."

But she noticed that some of the women seemed attracted to her ("I was the translator, and they were very dependent on me") and in retrospect realizes that she felt "a real interest" in a few of them.

"Some of the women were moving to Portland, and I decided to go check out Portland. I didn't really acknowledge why. I still wasn't saying I was a lesbian."

In Portland, however, where she became active in the women's movement, her denial lasted only a few months. And within a year, she and her then-partner accepted responsibility for a baby, a fifteen-month-old African American named Connie, born with fetal alcohol syndrome and abandoned by her biological mother. But the women's relationship didn't last, and Bonnie soon found herself a single custodial mother.

In 1975, she helped found and became the first director of the Bradley-Angle House (which continues in operation today, minus its founding director, as the oldest domestic violence agency on the West Coast). There, her first counselor was Sara Graham, and they became a couple two years later.

⌒

It was a union that many might have predicted could be headed for nowhere but disaster: The mothers were white and lesbian. Both children (Josh, ten, and Connie, six) were black. Each was firmly attached to its own mother and slow to warm to an outsider—Josh remembered his father, and Connie said she "already had another mother."

For some years, they basically presented themselves to the outside world as two families. Sara felt strongly that Josh had enough strikes against him—a black boy with a white mother, deeply shaken by the early death of his father—without the added pressure of having her known as a lesbian. And Josh wasn't ready to claim Connie as his sister.

"Here we were, to the outside just two single women with children," Bonnie says.

So it came as something of a shock to learn that however

hard they might try to stay closeted, they could not wholly shield Josh from discomfort with their status. An early revelation grew out of Josh's Little League participation. Bonnie liked baseball and loved attending his games with Sara, who but for Josh would not otherwise have been interested. But when Josh was about twelve, he asked Sara to start coming alone—people were beginning to ask questions about the woman with his mother.

Bonnie's initial reaction was to tell him that that wouldn't be fair to the rest of the family. But Sara was his primary parent, and she felt strongly that they should avoid adding homophobia to Josh's inescapable burden of racism.

That set the tone for Josh's growing up. Even at home, their relationship was never discussed.

Josh developed into a high school baseball star and a personal charmer with an eye for the girls. He "always had girls hanging around," Sara says, and "from eighth grade on, the telephone might as well have been his." Josh himself now concedes that his already vigorous teenage hormones were further fueled by a discomfort over his lesbian mothers that compelled him in a sense to flaunt his heterosexuality. "I felt like I had to prove my masculinity and that I was straight," he says. While several of his male friends visited regularly, he never brought any of his girl friends home. He often told others that Bonnie was his aunt.

For him, having a lesbian mother was harder than growing up black.

It wasn't until his early twenties, announcing that he

had fallen in love, that Josh for the first time introduced the women to a girl friend. The young woman, whom we'll call Teri (not her real name), became a frequent visitor and soon she and Josh were engaged. But from early on, Sara and Bonnie sensed that she was uneasy in their presence. Bonnie thought it might be because as an African American, Teri was not yet comfortable around white people. But finally, pressed by Sara, she openly expressed her deep aversion to their relationship. "I think it's gross and disgusting," she said.

Sara rightly feared that her attitude spelled future family woes, but Josh shrugged off Sara's worries. During one discussion, Sara happened to comment—a point obvious to her and she assumed to Josh—that "after all, there's nothing wrong with Bonnie and me."

Josh's reply would furnish the two women with the first of what they call their "bright light" or "aha" moments. "Well," he said, "there must be *something* wrong with it. You've never *talked* about it!"

"That nailed it," Bonnie says. "Our not talking about it had left him with no one to talk to. With no one to say 'It's okay,' he was left feeling that we must be ashamed, or else we would have talked abut it. We realized we had not spared him anything, that we had simply left him unprotected. I wish we had talked more openly, more directly about things."

Unknown to the two women, Josh had been often teased at school, and Teri was the first person he had ever really felt able to talk to about how hard that had been on him. For him, it brought a welcome sense of release, and he misinterpreted her response as primarily one of empathy for what he had gone through. It was a costly misunderstanding.

Only after they were engaged did Josh begin to suspect the full strength of Teri's antigay feelings and her antipathy toward Sara and Bonnie. But he told himself that would change.

The women strove to soften Teri's feelings—at one point enlisting the aid of a supportive African American heterosexual couple—but to no avail. And the strains predicted by Sara showed up early.

Within a year, Teri gave birth to a daughter, Cierra, whom Teri allowed Sara to see only infrequently and for the briefest of periods. Soon, Teri kept the baby from visiting the women altogether, but Josh surreptitiously stopped by often, sometimes at 6 AM on his way to drop her at day care.

Predictably, the marriage didn't last long. And even after they divorced, Teri's hostility toward Sara and Bonnie continued. Josh was forced to obtain a court order directing Teri to comply with their visitation agreement and allow Cierra to visit the women.

Josh says the problems with Teri "opened my eyes" to the virulent effects of prejudice. Until then, he says, Bonnie and Connie "weren't my family"—he hated the way, as he saw it, they had disrupted his life.

Sara and Bonnie now feel that by supporting Josh's urge to be mum about their relationship, they had merely reinforced his feelings of shame and left him open to the full brunt of homophobic pressure. Now two families were paying the price.

The good news was that Josh gained court ordered custody

of Cierra when she was eight, and she is now a cherished teenager whom the women describe as "the light of our lives" and an "absolutely delightful child," with features that are strikingly similar to those of her handsome father.

At thirty-seven, Josh is a department manager at one of Portland's largest retail firms, and lives with Cierra just around the corner from Bonnie and Sara. He is also the father, by another relationship, of a second daughter, five-year-old Maya, who stays with him regularly and, like Cierra, delights in visiting her grandmothers. With his admitted homophobia long dissolved, he also spends time as a volunteer with Bonnie's advocacy organization, Love Makes A Family. And he credits his nontraditional family with having, in the long run, supplied him with a deeply meaningful value system. The boy who once asked Bonnie to stay away from his baseball games has grown into a man who recently told *ABC News* and its nationwide audience, "There's so much love in our family."

It wasn't until Connie turned eighteen, and became legally empowered to grant permission for Bonnie to become her legal adoptive mother, that Bonnie could feel secure about her parental status. And until that happened, she felt constrained to keep a low profile as a lesbian, lest she lose custody of her daughter. So it was only after Connie's adoption, when Alex was six, that Bonnie gave full rein to her activist leanings.

For some years, she had nothing but a letter from

Connie's birth mother to support any parental rights. And it was addressed not to Bonnie but solely to her ex-partner, on the advice of a lawyer that naming two women could jeopardize whatever legal force the letter might otherwise have. The same lawyer advised against applying for adoption, lest it backfire and result in the court taking Connie away altogether and placing her in foster care. So Bonnie nervously applied instead for a legal guardianship, which carried no parental rights but at least would allow her to act on Connie's behalf, and she breathed somewhat easier when the probate court complied. Still, until Connie reached adulthood, clearing a safe path to adoption, Bonnie worried constantly about losing custody of her daughter.

She did not, however, have to worry, as with the boys, about Connie's reaction to antigay stigma. Connie simply never seemed to let that bother her while growing up. Today, herself a lesbian in her early thirties, Connie lives independently, and spends much of her time assisting needy neighbors by running errands for those who are elderly, caring for friends' pets, and otherwise helping wherever needed. Like Josh and Alex, she also volunteers at Love Makes A Family. Bonnie describes her as "solitary and independent" but also "a real people person, out and about doing what she can for others."

It was while Josh was in high school and Connie in middle school that Bonnie and Sara decided to have a third child with Bonnie as birth mother. The husband of a heterosexual couple with whom they were friendly, Leif Running, agreed to be the biological father—bicycling a jar of his sperm to the women's house, where Bonnie inseminated herself. So despite growing up in a home with two mothers, Alex has had no shortage of male role models. He cites Josh, sixteen years his senior, as his most significant role model. But he also remains close to Leif, with whom his relationship has passed through at least three separate phases. During his early school years, Alex saw a lot of him, but the tie only became genuinely close during Alex's teen years when, among other things, he often went hiking with Leif's family, helping sow the seeds of one of Alex's abiding adult passions, wilderness survival. Now, he says, his relationship with Leif is one of friendship more than father-and-son.

Alex's formative years contrast sharply with those of Josh in a variety of ways.

Josh's baseball stardom as a pitcher and general popularity had distracted him from serious study, for which Sara in part blames a school culture that failed to academically encourage top athletes, particularly those who were African American. Like Josh, Alex was always intellectually curious and precocious, but from the beginning more academically inclined. At the age of three, for example, he stunned Bonnie by complaining that her answer to one of his questions was "ambiguous"; when she asked him if he knew what that meant, he said, sure, it meant her answer "could mean either one thing or the other." It was a precursor of academic achievements to come.

More basic to his emotional development, however, was the change in his mothers' approach to their family's inevitable encounters with social prejudice.

They were now determined and, with Connie's status solidified, able to avoid secrecy about the nature of their relationship. So they could and did provide full family support for the cultural animosity they knew Alex would inevitably face.

Thus it was that Alex, at age eight, became himself a sort of junior warrior in the cultural warfare that descended on Oregon in 1992.

The origin of the statewide strife was the founding in the 1980s of the Oregon Citizens Alliance (OCA), a religion-oriented spin-off of the state's Republican Party. The OCA scored its first major triumph in 1988, when it sponsored an initiative that overturned an executive order banning discrimination in state hiring based on sexual orientation. In 1991, the organization found its full homophobic voice when it launched a petition drive promoting a ballot measure that would become Measure Nine in the 1992 general election.

To this day, the phrase "Measure Nine"—as in "during Measure Nine"—remains a familiar shorthand reference to the era of the vicious campaign and its aftermath that ravaged Oregon's gay community for several years. Measure Nine's mildest provisions called for the repeal of existing gay-rights ordinances in three cities and their outlaw elsewhere in the state. It went on to equate homosexuality with pedophilia, sadism, and masochism. If passed, it would establish as a constitutional tenet—and as required teaching in all the state's public schools and colleges—that homosexuality is "abnormal, wrong, unnatural, and perverse." The measure was so sweeping that, for example, physicians wondered whether it would mean that the University of Oregon School of Medicine could lose its accreditation because of its failure to teach that homosexuality was "perverse."

In the campaign fervor, a lesbian and a gay man were burned to death in Salem in an arson incident apparently triggered by antigay emotions. In Ashland, the openly supportive father of a gay man reported receiving a call from someone who told him, "Wouldn't it be nice if all homosexuals were dead?" Another father was told, "You ought to be ashamed to have a fucking queer son. . . . Does the bastard have AIDS yet?" The violence and threats of violence were worst in rural areas: in the small town of Grants Pass, an emergency room physician, openly supportive of his lesbian daughter, kept a loaded gun in his house for the first time in his life. "I was that scared," he said.

In Portland, with the full support of Sara, Bonnie had no qualms about opposing Measure Nine as an open lesbian.

"Josh had already been through all this stuff with Teri, and his wife had outed him to everybody he knew, so there was no concern about hurting him. Connie and Alex were already out to all of their friends. And I had been working for years with the Quakers to gain consensus about same-sex marriage, so I had a lot of experience talking to good-hearted people with Christian beliefs and culture."

Early on, she had become active in Alex's elementary school, "so that if anything was coming down the road, I would know about it and they would know me there as a real live person." Both before and after Measure Nine, her foresight would pay off.

Although Measure Nine itself was defeated, the OCA was heartened by its heavy support in rural areas and by the passage of a much tamer antigay resolution in Colorado the same day. Within months, the organization had launched a series of "Sons of Nine"—local ordinances banning civil rights protections for gays—with a view to undertaking another statewide initiative in 1994. In opposition, Bonnie not only stepped up her personal activism, but was joined by Alex, by now in middle school, less fearful of personal exposure and interested in becoming involved.

Bonnie, moreover, had become convinced that becoming involved was in his ultimate best interest—that it would help him "feel he had some power, and wasn't sitting back while people were bashing him." She explains:

"Alex had been through all the problems surrounding Josh's marriage. He had been through his own trauma with Nicole, the little girl next door. He had been around places where we had been talking about it openly for years. And I had made a decision that the only way to protect him was to teach him to fight for justice. I couldn't protect him, so he had better learn to fight for justice."

Alex in fact was the youngest of any of the youths willing to be visible in opposition to the OCA, participating in a variety of media appearances, including local TV shows and a *U.S. News & World Report* story on children with gay parents, complete with Alex's picture and quotes from Josh.

Perhaps Bonnie's proudest accomplishment during the era was initiating a resolution, in conjunction with the PTA president at Alex's school, which ultimately put the state Parent-Teacher Association on record in opposition to discrimination against parents, teachers, or students on the basis of sexual orientation.

During the ongoing ruckus over the "Son of Nine" initiatives, Alex accompanied Bonnie, and sometimes Sara, to some of the events. At one of them, a televised forum, he provided Bonnie with two more "bright light" moments.

The first came when Alex was asked on the show why he thought his mother should be allowed to marry her partner. His reply: "So that I won't be a bastard." To Bonnie, that was a new insight. By then, little stigma attached generally to children born out of wedlock but, "It was like our kids were the new bastards."

After the forum, while waiting outside for Sara to pick them up, Bonnie and Alex found themselves standing with Scott Lively, the principal OCA spokesman, who engaged Bonnie in a Biblical debate about homosexuality. She responded with confidence and gusto ("As a minister's daughter, I had always felt an absolute obligation to win all the Bible verse contests.")—but also with calm and, she hoped, compassion. In the car, Alex asked why she had been so nice to Lively:

"He was telling you that you shouldn't have had me. But what he was really saying is that I shouldn't have been born."

Bonnie says of that second "aha" moment of the evening: "It really hit me that the message to children of lesbian and gay relationships was worse than the message to their parents."

———

Alex's media appearances spread awareness of his family situation beyond his personal friends to the entire student body of his middle school. One immediate result was an increase in the slurs from school mates. That in turn would lead to the fist fight that resulted in his suspension from school.

For a time, Alex refused to respond to the upsurge in taunts. But he reached the limits of his patience on a day that began with a personal triumph, when his model race car, built with infinite care and patience over several weeks, came in first in a school contest.

On the school bus that afternoon, one of the race car competitors, perhaps out of simple envy, teased the winner about his family: "Your mother is a lezzie." The remark pierced Alex's wall of restraint and he proceeded, as he would later phrase it on national television, to "beat the crap" out of his taunter.

Both boys were suspended from school and prohibited from attending an upcoming school dance. Alex was heartbroken and, pressed by his mother, told her how it had happened, as well as about other incidents of harassment that he hadn't previously mentioned. Bonnie was disappointed that her son had gotten into a fight, but also angered by the school's tolerance of such harassment.

With a friend, Bonnie raised the matter with the principal, Peter Hamilton. She describes him as "a good man" who understood the evils of discrimination and who would soon become the chair of all the city's middle school principals—but who had never considered this particular problem. He pointed out that the staff by now included some gay and lesbian members. To which Bonnie replied:

"I see you have a picture of your wife and family on your desk. Do they [the gay staff members] have pictures of *their* partners on their desks? I see you're wearing a wedding ring, advertising your heterosexuality. Do they advertise *their* orientation?"

To Bonnie's delight, the very next school bulletin to parents included an article by Hamilton, announcing a school policy of zero tolerance for harassment based on sexual orientation.

Bonnie thinks it is critical for the well-being of their children that same-sex parents go public with their personal stories:

"It's from these stories that people connect with us and realize that we're just people like they are, parents like they are, and families like they are. Then they can move to a place where they don't want to hurt our kids."

And she knows that Portland is now a far friendlier place for gays and lesbians generally, as well as for the children of so many of them, because of the public education ("We *had* to talk about this stuff") triggered by the Measure Nine and "Sons of Nine" campaigns.

Few in the city would disagree—to the presumably everlasting dismay of the Oregon Citizens Alliance.

Now, as a college senior, Alex says that having lesbian mothers is just one of the critical influences on his personal identity. Also important is the fact that he grew up in a low-income family (Bonnie's modest and irregular salary as executive director of Love Makes A Family is to this day a primary source of family income), with many black friends in a predominantly black neighborhood, and with a black older brother as a primary role model. (In Bonnie's words, "He felt he grew up a culturally African American in a white boy's skin.") Thus, in a mostly upper class white high school, he was "thinking black and poor," which further underscored his differences from others in his daily school routine.

Throughout most of high school, in order to earn more spending money to keep pace with his wealthy school friends, Alex worked as much as twenty hours a week at a Borders book store coffee shop, in addition to spending time in the Love Makes A Family office. At one point, Bonnie volunteered to quit the organization and get a job that would pay more, but he objected: "You can't do that. Love Makes A Family is too important." Because he worked Friday nights, he missed most of the high school dances—a major sacrifice for any teenager with average adolescent hormones but especially to one driven to "prove" his heterosexuality, because of his "gay" family. As he told Barbara Walters on *20/20*, "I definitely wanted to show, 'Hey guys, I like girls. . . . I'm not like that just because my mom is.'"

To a question from Walters, he replied that he and his current girlfriend had been together exactly six months. She joshed, "Six whole months today, huh?" To which

Alex replied, "I'm seventeen. It's a big deal." And in fact, four years later, as I write, he and the same girl are considering the possibility of a lifetime commitment.

⁓

During the 1990s ideological wars, in one of her numerous radio and television appearances, Bonnie debated OCA spokesman Scott Lively on a conservative Christian radio station in Vancouver, Washington, across the Columbia River from Portland. The experience convinced her that such a station was the right venue for her: "Their listeners are who I want to talk to. I'm not that interested in going on an alternative station and talking to everybody who agrees with me."

So she applied to the owner, a Vancouver woman, for a talk show spot. The owner was at first reluctant, but agreed when one of her regular hosts, an evangelical preacher, backed Bonnie by saying, "I don't think Jesus would want people hating gays the way they do."

Presumably to play it safe, the owner gave her a half-hour slot "at a time nobody was likely to hear it anyway." But the response was encouraging, and the station allowed her to buy a weekly slot during the coveted 7–9 AM commute hours. Her show, like her advocacy organization, was known as *Love Makes A Family*, and she funded it with ads and contributions that she generated herself. It lasted four years, until the station was taken over by a new owner she found difficult to work with.

Meanwhile, her style reflected her heritage of reasoned, nonviolent activism. As one writer put it, Bonnie "will employ her calming vocal tones in an attempt to find out why a caller feels the way he or she does . . . vitriol is never part of the formula."

One frequent caller was a woman named Laura who claimed to have been threatened by three bisexuals she said were "serial killers."

"My goodness. That's a lot of serial killers for one person to run across in their life," Bonnie responded, her irony lost on the caller.

Bonnie had little ultimate success with Laura, but with others, as phrased by *TLN Magazine:* "In the same way a police officer tries to disarm a hostage taker, Tinker negotiates with her callers in order to get what she wants."

In one instance, for example, a caller named Jim complained about gays walking "naked at the gay parades." Bonnie pointed out that he was in fact referring to a single woman who took her shirt off on a blistering hot day, and when Jim paused, Bonnie added:

"But did you see everyone else at the parade? All of those families who were marching . . . and playing with their kids on the swings. Just like at the Rose Festival [a major annual civic event in Portland]—families coming out to spend fun time together."

Jim's indignation seemed to fade.

⌒

That *20/20* show, of course, marked the high tide of media publicity about the family. It also led to some serious disagreement with the *20/20* staff—an episode that despite the generally gay-friendly tone of the show reflects some of the other undercurrents of prejudice in American culture.

Bonnie and Sara were hesitant when the show's producers first approached them about their family being included in their projected piece on children of same-sex parents. But the producers persisted, saying they were particularly interested because of the diversity of the family: children who came into the family through birth and adoption, who were both black and white, and one of whom was herself lesbian. They sent a crew to Portland for a full weekend, filming the entire family, including shots of Alex with his friends, running track and at his job, and others of Bonnie and Sara at the courthouse registering as domestic partners. Then the network flew both Josh and Alex to New York, where they sat side by side being interviewed by Walters.

So it was that the resulting TV version came as a shock to the family. As Bonnie tells it:

"There was absolutely nothing in it of Josh, Connie, or Cierra, no picture of our whole, family, no mention that there was anyone else in our family. We were very excited, and then when it finally came out, you would have thought we were two white moms with one white boy.

"Josh was just devastated, because he had told his friends he was going to be on it. And it was upsetting to Alex, both because of what they had done to Josh and because so many of his closest friends were African American.

"We knew they would do some editing, but we hadn't realized they had just totally wiped him out. It was really embarrassing to us, because race has impacted our lives as much as anything. And Josh was the one who came first and bore the brunt of the discrimination, making it easier for Alex."

They voiced their objections to one of the producers, who admitted they didn't want to "complicate" Alex's story by including the other family members. But they agreed to edit the piece for a rerun version, and the video of the program now includes one shot of Josh, a picture of the entire family, and a reference to Alex having an older brother. In addition, the network posted on its Web site a story about both the boys, "Young Men With Gay Moms," which included the essential facts about both their lives.

But no one, least of all Bonnie or Sara, could take issue with the ABC producer who said their family story was "complicated." Josh sums it up:

"The experience was hard but I wouldn't trade it for anything in the world. Just the experience of living in a different family teaches you a lot of values."

2.

Families at Sea—and on the Cape

On July 11, 2004, the liner *Norwegian Dawn* sailed from New York for the Caribbean with more than sixteen hundred passengers made up of gay and lesbian parents and their nearly six hundred children, plus extended family members and friends. It was the same ship that Republican Senate Majority Leader Tom DeLay, a fierce opponent of gay marriage, had proposed using as a luxury entertainment center for that summer's Republican National Convention. To DeLay's presumed dismay, bipartisan criticism had scotched his plan.

A week later, when the *Dawn* docked on its return,

DeLay perhaps would have been even more shocked to hear an announcement by the captain over the ship intercom. He had never experienced a cruise, the captain told his voyagers, with more well behaved children or more attentive parents.

However well behaved, the kids also had their fill of noisy fun. There were the usual on-board amusements, games, and swimming, and island stops with sight-seeing, snorkeling, parasailing, scuba diving, and more.

But for many, the biggest thrill came simply from meeting and bonding with droves of other young people from similar families. (A perhaps common first query: "What do you have, two dads or two moms?" One possible answer: "Two moms *and* a dad.") They eagerly traded stories and tips about survival in school, who to tell and not to tell about their families, and how to answer the "dumb questions" of others.

Perhaps best of all, they basked in the comfort of being wholly surrounded by people, old and young, with whom they could let down the guards they employed daily at home.

The cruise was the kickoff event of R Family Vacations, an organizational brainchild of travel promoter Gregg Kaminsky, celebrity Rosie O'Donnell and O'Donnell's mate Kelli Carpenter O'Donnell, co-parent of their four children. With them on the *Dawn* was Kelli's mother, Melanie Safer, one of numerous grandmothers seen during the week pushing infants in strollers—in Melanie Safer's case, Kelli's biological daughter Vivian ("Vivi"). (In Rosie's first stand-up routine in the ship's theater, she unleashed a barrage of mother-in-law jabs that drew roars of laughter, with the good-natured Safer laughing as hard as any.)

But behind all the hullabaloo was some serious business, as parents exchanged stories of dealing with the "real" world and attended a variety of on-board seminars and workshops designed to help them cope with that world's gay-hostile attitudes.

Most of the workshops were put on by the Family Pride Coalition, an international organization of families headed by same-sex parents observing its twenty-fifth anniversary that summer. To Aimee Gelnaw, then in the waning months of a four-year term as the Coalition's executive director, the joy of families meeting with others like their own was nothing new. Nor, even with sixteen hundred people aboard, would the cruise mark the year's largest gathering for the Coalition. That distinction would fall just two weeks later, when additional hundreds would flock to an annual Coalition event on Cape Cod.

A 1950s pop hit of singer Patti Page, revived on a 1998 album by Bette Midler, praises the charms of "Old Cape Cod." Those wooed by such features as sand dunes and "quaint little villages," it predicts, are "sure to fall in love with Old Cape Cod."

The song might strike a chord, as it were, with the some two thousand members of same sex parented families who vacation each summer at the Family Pride Coalition's Family Week at the tip of the Cape in Provincetown,

Massachusetts. But for the most part, the families' love of Old Cape Cod is likely to have little to do with the qualities popularized by Page and Midler.

The principal attraction to those families, sand dunes and quaint villages notwithstanding, stems from some intensely personal connections: excited conversations with new and old friends, exchanges of experiences and ideas, and, in the midst of one of America's vacation playgrounds, endless hours of workshops.

"It's really quite amazing," says Corri Planck, the Coalition's director of advocacy, communications and support. "It happened on the cruise and it happens at our Family Weeks at Provincetown, Saugatuck [Michigan], and Palm Springs. These are great vacation spots, but people have such a hunger for conversation that they want to go to workshops.

"And they always say, 'We wish this could go on longer so we could continue this discussion.'"

Talk to any parent or child who has taken part in the Coalition's Family Week events, and they'll tell you the occasions are lifelines for their families.

For example, Danielle Silber (see chapter 7) grew up in a community relatively accustomed to her kind of nontraditional family; her mothers made certain she knew and played with children from similar families; and she experienced virtually no overt harassment in her early years for having two mothers. Still, the cultural stigma was as part of the air she breathed, and for years she was uncomfortable and secretly ashamed of her family—until 1998, when the family first went to Provincetown.

"It was the first time I was surrounded by a lot of

other kids in a similar situation to mine," she remembers. "It was the first time I could talk openly about the fear and the pain and the shame. People understood. They got it. It was just incredible to be in a room with people who could totally understand your experience."

⁓

Aimee Gelnaw became executive director of Family Pride Coalition in 2001. Herself the mother of two children—the older of whom has been attending Family Week since its inception in 1996 when he was eleven—she describes it as lifesaving for many of the kids.

"It's the one week in the year they're not a minority, when they feel safe to talk about their families. And they blossom.

"The best part of my job is watching kids like Danielle grow up. Our events have a family reunion quality, where everybody sees how the kids are growing up and changing. It's a community experience with a very enriching and stabilizing influence."

In 2004, Provincetown's Family Week officially hosted 425 families. Individual workshops drew as many as seventy participants, averaging about thirty-five a session, who displayed what Corri Planck describes as the "hunger" to learn and to work with others in similar families.

The Provincetown Family Week was one of six similar events organized or participated in by the Coalition during the year. A few weeks earlier, a Family Week at Saugatuck drew a smaller gathering of about forty-five families. Other annual events in 2004 included a Family Camp in Newton, New Jersey; a weekend at Disney World in Orlando, Florida; and an October gathering in Palm Springs ("Our Families in the Desert") for some sixty families.

Back in her office in Washington, D.C., where the Coalition has been headquartered since 2002, Gelnaw, for four years (until 2005) headed a staff of six that, not surprisingly, deals with far more than organizing exciting events.

In a society generally hostile to same-sex parents, the Coalition's battle agenda never runs thin.

⁓

Anne Magro and Heather Finstuen are the parents of twin girls born in 1998 to Magro and adopted by Heather by second parent adoption when the family lived in New Jersey. Partners since 1991, the women now live in Norman, Oklahoma, where Anne teaches accounting at the University of Oklahoma. Members of Family Pride Coalition, they and their daughters have attended both the Coalition Family Camp in New Jersey and the Family Week in Saugatuck.

Now, the family is among the scores of thousands of families victimized by the antigay backlash touched off by the 2004 Massachusetts decision legalizing gay marriage in that state. In Oklahoma, the frenzy of hostility produced a law that strips Heather of any claim to parenthood, by nullifying second parent adoptions from other states when the parents are in Oklahoma. (It declares that the state "shall not recognize an adoption by more than one individual of the same sex from any other state or foreign jurisdiction.")

With the Coalition's assistance, Anne and Heather have become plaintiffs in a suit brought by Lambda Legal that claims the law is unconstitutional as a denial of equal protection and violation of the Constitution's Full Faith and Credit clause.

In a Coalition press release, Heather explained some of the concerns created by the drastic law:

"I worry about being allowed to parent my children, from doctors' visits to school field trips and everything in between. What would happen to the girls if Anne died tomorrow—would Oklahoma . . . come take the girls away from me?"

Meanwhile, more mundane concerns haunt the couple's everyday life. What happens if one of the girls needs emergency care while Anne is at work—would a hospital be required to turn the child away because Heather has no parental rights to approve treatment or medical care? Heather presumably is barred from signing legal forms of any kind on behalf of her daughters—even from chaperoning school events.

"We are a family," Heather says. "Anne and I made a decision to raise children together and with that decision came the responsibility to protect them as much as we can. Oklahoma should respect my adoption. Instead, they are putting my children at risk."

Also plaintiffs in the case are Ed Swaya and Greg Hampel, who live in Washington State, where they legally adopted a girl, Vivian, born to an Oklahoma woman. Even before the new law was passed, the Oklahoma State

Department of Health at first balked at issuing a corrected birth certificate showing the two men as Vivian's parents. It finally did so, but the men say that even with the corrected certificate, the passage of the new law leaves them afraid to bring Vivian to visit her birth mother in Oklahoma.

"If Vivian were hurt, would an Oklahoma hospital recognize Greg and me as her lawful parents?" asks Swaya. "I'm not prepared to take that risk. I have a very real fear that as a parent I wouldn't be able to make critical decisions for my daughter when she needs me the most."

Another case that prompted a Coalition initiative was that of seven-year-old Marcus McLaurin in Lafayette, Louisiana.

On a November day in 2003, Marcus was in line waiting to go to recess at Ernest Gallet Elementary School, when the boy next to him asked him about his father. Marcus said he didn't have a father, he had two mothers.

"You can't have two moms!"

"Well, I do"

"How come?"

"Because my mother is gay."

"What does that mean?"

"Gay is when a girl likes another girl."

Their teacher overheard the conversation, pulled Marcus out of line, scolded him in front of the class for using a bad word, and sent him to the principal's office in lieu of recess. The principal ordered him to attend a special 6:45 AM behavioral clinic the following week, where he would be forced to repeatedly write, "I will never use the word 'gay' in school again." The assistant principal called his mother, Sharon Huff.

"He told me my son had said a word so bad that he didn't want to repeat it over the phone," Sharon told lawyers at the American Civil Liberties Union. "But that was nothing compared to the shock I felt when my little boy came home and told me that his teacher had told him his family is a dirty word.

"No child should ever hear that, especially not from a teacher he trusted and respected."

Marcus had to fill out a "student behavior contract form" on which he wrote that he misbehaved because he "sed bad wurds." At the top of the form, the teacher wrote, "He explained to another child that you are gay and what being gay means." On a behavior report signed by the assistant principal, the teacher wrote, "Marcus decided to explain to another child in his group that his mom is gay. He told the other child that gay is when a girl likes a girl. This kind of discussion is not acceptable in my room. I feel that parents should explain things of this nature to their children in their own way."

In addition to all the denigration among his school-mates, teachers and administrators, Marcus lost one of his closest playmates, a friend who lived next door but whose parents now no longer allowed him to play with Marcus.

The ACLU sent the principal a letter explaining that the disciplinary actions were unconstitutional and asking the school to remove all mentions of the incident from Marcus's record, to refrain from restricting his speech in the future, and to apologize to Marcus and his mother. The school failed to respond, but Marcus's mothers decided not to take the case to court and risk further harmful exposure for Marcus.

In Washington, Aimee Gelnaw and the Coalition staff were understandably appalled when they heard Marcus's story. Aimee says:

"The message given to this kid is the word 'gay' is bad and you can never speak about your parents in school.

"Imagine that: The language he needs to talk about the people he loves most in the world are bad words. And the message to all of the kids in the school is the same, with all its implications about devaluing his family."

She says Coalition members from all over the country "were calling in, writing in, asking, 'What can we do?'" They felt powerless, tied to their jobs and homes, unable to go to Louisiana to take part in protests and demonstrations there.

"When people hear something like this, their hearts are breaking, thinking, 'This could be my kids.' It's such a personal thing, they felt an incredible desire to participate in some way.

"We talked about how fortunate we are, that we are actually doing something about this kind of thing. It empowers us in a way that others don't feel in these situations."

So, while they could do nothing to help Marcus directly, the staff searched for ways to enable their members to take positive action and feel that same sense of empowerment. The result was a "Send Our Families to School" campaign, encouraging and assisting members to undertake book drives to contribute informative, positive books to their children's schools and libraries. Gelnaw describes such local activities as "small steps that individuals can do that make a difference."

"Lots of people responded to that and we got lots of positive reports back. We know our parents are really busy, raising children, holding jobs, and facing the added challenge of raising their children in a world that isn't always very hospitable. So as an organization, we're always trying to find ways to empower them, to give them opportunities to make a difference, and feel they have a voice in creating change."

Over the years, the Coalition has in fact seen a sea change not only in the attitudes of the general public, but in those of the gay community itself. At first, the gay community generally didn't welcome families and Provincetown was wholly unprepared for the Coalition's first gathering of thirty-five families. Now, it's one of "P-Town's" summer highlights.

"Even the stock in the town stores changes," Gelnaw told a reporter. "You see a lot more diapers on the shelves."

3.

Gay Dads Who "Really, Really, Really" Wanted to Be Parents

When Hope Steinman-Iacullo turned five, her fathers Wayne Steinman and Sal Iacullo decided it was time she saw Disney World. They set out on a Labor Day weekend from their Staten Island, New York, home and soon were passing through Virginia on I-95. Wayne was driving; Sal was in the back seat entertaining Hope.

Nearing Richmond, they stopped at a diner for lunch. As they sat down, a state patrolman entered, walked to their table, and began to question Sal—on suspicion of kidnapping!

Gay male fathers were then virtually unheard of. Wayne and Sal are white and Hope is biracial. They had not thought to bring her adoption papers. The officer was skeptical of the explanation that they were just a family on a Disney World outing. Their vision of the Magic Kingdom was dissolving into that of the county jail. Then a confused Hope saved the day by addressing her questions to "Daddy Wayne" and "Daddy Sal."

Sal asked the patrolman what had caused him to suspect kidnapping.

"You were in the back seat obviously trying to keep the child quiet," said the officer.

"Yes, that's what parents do," replied a miffed Sal.

~

It was the second day at sea of the R Family Cruise (see chapter 2), when Sal told his story to a standing-room-only crowd of some forty men in a meeting room of the liner *Norwegian Dawn*. Ranging in age from the twenties to fifties, they were there for a seminar entitled "Being a Dad in a Mom's World." At least two of them were young men currently without partners but who nonetheless knew they wanted to be parents. Several of the others were also "wannabe" parents. But more than half were already parents, a few of teenagers.

The ensuing discussion ranged through a variety of topics from adoption to surrogacy to infant colic, and down to such nitty-gritty as utilizing Federal Express for shipping a surrogate mother's milk. At times, inevitably, the talk turned to dealing with the potential for school and cultural hostility. Most reported only minor difficulties. But a Texas father told of a kindergarten teacher who had forced his son to make a Mother's Day card, and to sit apart from the rest of the class for some weeks.

A wannabe raised the less weighty matter of what the dads were called by their kids. One said his son as a teenager had finally solved the knotty problem by calling his biological father "Dad" and his second parent "Uncle Mame."

Perhaps for most, more valuable than the answers to their specific questions was the aura of comfort and confidence exuded by the two couples who led the discussion: Sal, Wayne, and Tim Fisher and Scott Davenport of Bethesda, Maryland. The four men were true pioneers on the 1980s frontier of gay male parenting.

Also on board and featured on several of the cruise programs was a gay dad pioneer of a different sort: Esara Tuaolo, the third-ever former National Football League player to out himself as gay. Tuaolo, a nine year NFL veteran who played in the 1999 Super Bowl, is also a talented singer and has described himself as "just your typical gay Samoan ex-nose tackle in show business."

Closeted by necessity during his football career, Esara says he deeply envied the joy he saw on the faces of his married teammates with their families. But now, with the man he always refers to as his husband, Mitchell Wherley, he shares that joy as the adoptive father of four-year-old twins, Mitchell, Jr. and Michelle.

On the ship, Tuaolo charmed and moved audiences with his robust singing style and his poignant story of a fatherhood delayed by a brand of homophobia probably nowhere more vicious than in professional sports.

The three couples followed different paths to fatherhood. But they all demonstrate the conclusions of New
York University Sociologist Dr. Judith Stacey. Propor-
tionally, she notes, fewer gay men than lesbians decide to
become parents, and it's obviously more difficult for
them to do so. So they tend to be extremely dedicated,
superior parents, in part because even more than lesbians they necessarily have to "really, really, really want
to be parents."

Wayne Steinman and Sal Iacullo

Wayne says his first love letter from Sal, in 1972, mentioned Sal's interest in having children.

"I thought he was crazy," Wayne says. "You never saw
children in the gay male community. And I actually
thought not having kids was one of the benefits of being
gay—you didn't have to.

"So I just brushed it off and said 'Okay, Sal, anything
you say.' Because I didn't think he could be serious."

Wayne was twenty-two, Sal twenty-three. Both had
only recently started their first jobs, both as teachers at
a school for the mentally retarded. So having a child was
not at that point a realistic expectation in any event. But
by the mid-'80s, Wayne had become New York City
Comptroller Harrison Goldin's liaison to the gay community, Sal was working for the New York City Department of Mental Health, and they had moved to an
apartment with an extra bedroom. So when a social services organization asked them to put up a young man

thrown out of his home because he was gay, and who needed a place to stay for a few days, they agreed. The few days became more than a year, and the youth, Joey, triggered some latent parental feelings in Wayne:

"We hit it off so well that we told him he could stay with us for as long as he wanted. And during the time he was with us, all these parenting urges came up in me. I was quite surprised." Until then, he speculates, such feelings had simply been strongly suppressed. Sal had always been the one to press for parenthood and would in fact turn out to take the primary nurturing role with their own child. But by the time Joey left, Wayne was as avid a wannabe parent as Sal.

A year and a half later, Sal would become New York City's first openly gay adoptive parent. And some years after that, once it became possible under New York law, Wayne would proudly add his name, as "Parent Number Two," to Hope's birth certificate.

⁓

For two openly gay men in 1986, the route to parenthood was wholly uncharted. A few gay and lesbian parent groups existed, but were made up of men and women who had become parents while formerly married.

For most couples who, like Wayne and Sal, weren't insisting on the perfectly healthy white infant, there was an abundance of available children. But they knew that being openly gay could be a barrier. They also knew they couldn't do it any other way. Wayne says:

"That's how we had always lived our lives up to that

point. We had never made any apologies about it and didn't feel this was the time to start. We were particularly certain that we didn't ever want to give a child a mixed message that there might be something wrong with being gay.

"So we were very lucky. We happened into the right place at the right time with the right people."

Ironically, the "right" place and people turned out to be at Little Flower Children's Services, a Catholic Charity agency affiliated with the Brooklyn diocese.

They attended an orientation session there, but assumed they were wasting their time. When the social worker completed her presentation, Sal asked—"though we knew the answer"—whether the society had any religious affiliation. To their surprise, as Wayne recalls:

"She saw the two men sitting together, got the picture right away, and knew exactly where the question was coming from. Her first words were, 'We do not discriminate on the basis of sexual orientation, gender, physical handicap or religion.' Almost as an afterthought, she added, 'And oh, yes, we are affiliated with the church.'"

"That set the tone. We had absolutely no problems with them."

They heard indirectly that they had triggered some uneasiness behind the scenes at Little Flower. But the social workers they worked with went out of their way to be helpful, and they were soon certified as qualified adoptive parents.

Beyond Little Flower, the route proved more difficult. The men spent eight months encountering twenty-four consecutive rejections from other adoption agencies in the search for an actual child. Some of the refusals were clearly justified—where, for example, a child needed to be near her siblings in another part of the state. But in other instances homophobia was clearly at work, the most glaring example being that of a boy whose requirements called specifically for a strong male presence.

They were so frustrated that they were considering filing a class action suit when they got a call from Little Flower offering them a four-month-old girl born to a Latina woman, thought to be Puerto Rican, and a black father.

The girl's mother, a cocaine user, had abandoned her at birth. The infant had tremors typical of a drug syndrome, poor muscular development and what the men were told was a possibility of permanent disability conditions. Confidentiality rules barred practitioners who had seen the girl from providing full medical details.

Given just twenty-four hours to decide, and wholly confused by what they had been told, they said they wanted to meet the child in order to make up their minds.

"We saw Hope on a Friday and we fell in love immediately," Wayne recounts. "We knew as soon as they brought her into the room, despite the fact that she was wrapped in tons of pink polyester, that this was our child. She related to us. And we knew that whatever issues were there, we could deal with it.""

Sal echoes the point: "I knew Hope belonged to us. We said, 'Yes, this is our child.'"

On Monday, accompanied by Wayne's mother and both of Sal's parents, they went to the office where Hope was placed in their arms. They took her to the home of Sal's parents, where Wayne's mother and Sal's sisters and brother with their three children (two of them only a few months older than Hope) joined in a family celebration of Hope's homecoming. It had all happened so quickly that the grandparents then had to take the new dads on an emergency shopping run for furniture and other necessities.

Hope's ailments proved to be relatively minor, evidently the result of prenatal drug exposure, aggravated by being confined to a crib for virtually all of her twenty-seven days in a hospital and three months in foster care. She had apparently been kept well cleaned and fed. But a bald spot on the back of her head suggested she had spent minimal time in anyone's arms.

A neurologist and physical therapist prescribed what they would have done anyway—play with her and encourage activities to strengthen her muscles. Within months, Hope was fully healthy.

It was clear from the outset that Sal would be the primary nurturer. Wayne says he "does the chores"— cleaning the windows, shopping, gardening and so on.

During the long months of their search, they had tried to think through every issue they might face as parents. Now, with a child actually in place, they had to deal with the one that loomed as perhaps their biggest hurdle, and remains so even today.

Ironically, it was the same matter that divides many heterosexual couples—religion. Sal is devoutly Catholic. Wayne is Jewish, observes Jewish holidays, and felt he wanted to "pass along the culture" even though he doesn't consider himself very religious. But however mild his formal devotion to Judaism, he had "very strong opinions against the Catholic religion."

It had been an intensely divisive issue throughout the search process. Now, Wayne reluctantly consented to raising Hope Catholic, reconciling his decision with the thought that "she would get exposure to Judaism from me and my family." But there was also a quite practical reason for him to concede the point. In 1987, state law permitted only one of the men to adopt, and Sal was the obvious choice; he had a permanent civil service job with fixed benefits, whereas Wayne was a political appointee, his job subject to the whim of the voters. (It would in fact end after just six years, when Comptroller Goldin was roundly defeated in a primary run for mayor.) And if Sal was the legal parent, Wayne felt it only made sense to respect Sal's religion. (Wayne wouldn't legally become a parent until 1995, after New York's second parent adoption procedure took effect.)

Wayne's entire family attended Hope's baptism, but Wayne says he privately "refused to acknowledge" what was happening. And after her first communion, he could no longer contain his objections. He told Sal he couldn't allow her to be confirmed. They had a major row and this time it was Sal who conceded.

But Sal immediately sank into depression. Wayne says, "He felt he was breaking all the vows he had taken to assure Hope's religious upbringing. His mental change was so severe that two weeks later, I ended up giving in again."

As time passed, it was Sal who assured that Hope's Catholicism was embellished by knowledge of Judaism and its customs, and they celebrated Chanukah and Passover along with Christmas and Easter. Of most importance to the dads was that Hope's childhood was enriched by family traditions.

⁓

Hope now speaks regularly before a variety of groups on the pleasures and perils of having gay dads. At one recent panel before a mixed gay-and-straight crowd, she described Wayne and Sal as "amazing parents" who "gave me the confidence to develop into my own person."

Wayne and Sal had their work cut out for them in Staten Island, which in general does not too readily welcome diversity. But the men have always been up-front in all respects, pursuing a sort of "the-best-defense-is-a-good-offense" philosophy. Sal likes to tell one story about shopping in a local department store with the infant Hope in his arms. When a diaper change became urgent, he asked a clerk where he could do it. There were facilities in the ladies' room, she said. He told her that wouldn't do, and the clerk huffily said she just couldn't help him.

"We happened to be right next to the furniture department," Sal says. "So I just laid her down on a bed and changed her. The clerk had a fit, but I told her, 'Until you make accommodations for me, this is where I have to do it.'" (Most department stores have of course since made just such accommodations—even if not with gay men in mind.)

More importantly, their up-front attitude insured that the nature of Hope's family would have minimal effect on her school environment. She doesn't recall a single other schoolmate with gay parents. But she says her fathers smoothed her way by their active involvement not only at school, but also with her friends and her friends' parents. Wayne in turn explains their longtime stance:

"We've found that if on the first meeting you get rid of all the questions, all the things people might gossip about behind your back, it becomes a nonissue. We garner respect by respecting ourselves.

"So you always know we're Wayne and Sal. We're a gay couple. We'll give you our life histories if you want to hear it. We live our lives in a visible way where people can see we are no different than they are."

So despite the general societal homophobia, Hope says she always found school "a nurturing environment where I didn't feel threatened." She's particularly grateful for the fact the dads were always comfortable with her friends and made a point of becoming friends with their parents.

But the added pressures are always there, for both parents and child.

As to the dads, Wayne says, "We feel like we're under a microscope, that everybody's waiting for that first slipup, and that we have to work on a level 110 to 120 percent in order to be the perfect parents."

Substitute "child" for "parent" and the point res-
onates at least as strongly with Hope. She talks about the
pressures that come from "the fears and myths" of conventional wisdom: "Oh, my God, you're going to turn
out horribly. Your parents are going to make you gay.
You must have psychological problems.

"So there's pressure to show that you're just perfect.
Well, the reality is that no family is perfect. Whether
you have gay or straight parents, every family has its
problems."

If Hope had no schoolmates with gay parents, she
never lacked for knowing numerous families like hers.
Before she was even a year old, Wayne and Sal helped
found Center Kids, a gay parenting group still functioning at New York City's LGBT community center.
From the time she was three, they attended family
events of the Gay and Lesbian Parents Coalition International (now the Family Pride Coalition), where over
the years she would eventually come to meet scores of
other children with same-sex parents.

Wayne and Sal meanwhile helped form a variety of
family groups, including one (in conjunction with Tim
Fisher and Scott Davenport, see below) limited just to
gay men. Wayne was a member of the Coalition board
for five years and its president from 1997 to 1999. He
also has put together various Coalition materials for
wannabe parents, including two guides, "Lesbian and
Gay Parenting Resource Directory" and "Adoption
Reading Packet."

Before Hope entered any school, her fathers introduced themselves and explained the family makeup to

all of her teachers and administrators. Both became PTA presidents, Wayne during elementary school and Sal in middle school, and Sal chaired a School Leadership Team. By design, Sal's office was just two blocks from her elementary school and middle school, and he became personally friendly with the principal. He confesses to becoming a regular presence the staff simply could not ignore. Once Hope reached high school, the men decided to be less directly involved in school affairs, and Sal admits, "I had trouble doing that."

Hope was in classes for the gifted by fourth grade, and has always been an honor student. She's outspoken, an all-around high achiever, and in Wayne's words, "very politically aware" with "a very strong social consciousness." Since she was ten, every summer the family has attended the Family Pride Coalition's annual Family Week on Cape Cod, and Hope has become a board member of COLAGE (Children of Lesbians and Gays Everywhere), a national Family Pride offshoot.

She's now a high school senior, and her dads see her as something of a college admissions officer's dream because of her combination of academic excellence, racial and cultural diversity, political and social awareness and activism, and her involvement with COLAGE. Wayne says admissions officers' eyes light up at that COLAGE directorship: "It shows leadership ability besides the smarts."

In a discussion with me, he described her as definitely heterosexual. Later, talking with Hope, I told her what Wayne had said. She agreed that while she's "always been attracted to guys," she didn't like the term "definitely." "I feel sexual orientation is something that is fluid."

She resents the pressure placed on her and others like her—coming at least as strongly from gays as from straights—to "prove" that she is heterosexual:

"I'm primarily attracted to men, and that's fine. But I don't like labels and I don't like the feeling of having to prove my heterosexuality. I don't like having to fit into labels. I think life is more complex than that."

Like many children of gay parents, she finds that her affinity with queer culture marks a significant difference between her and the average teenager: "I grew up in the queer culture. I'm entirely comfortable around queer people. That's my community as well, and where I feel safe."

Her dads feel her life will probably be easier as a heterosexual than if she were gay. But they say they never feared as she was growing up, as do many gay parents, the possibility that she might be homosexual.

"Personally," says Wayne, "I say who better to raise gay kids than gay parents? We allow our children to express themselves and be themselves. And we've lived through the issues."

Another matter they are necessarily leaving to her is the one that has always conflicted her fathers—the question of religion. In accord with Wayne's concession, Hope was confirmed in the Catholic Church. But now she herself differs with many of the Church's theological and political positions, although she has not formally renounced her faith and continues to take communion occasionally.

Her fathers say they are "confident she will find some way to celebrate her spirituality."

Wayne is now a contract administrator with the New York City Department of Health and Mental Hygiene. Sal is the director of adult day services for a Brooklyn social service agency serving the developmentally disabled.

They were legally married in Toronto, Canada in 2003 with Hope at their side. And three years earlier, they held a formal wedding ceremony in Vermont celebrating the recognition of their civil union in that state.

At the ceremony, the best man was the son of some close friends.

And the maid of honor was a beaming twelve-year-old Hope Steinman-Iacullo.

Tim Fisher and Scott Davenport

Fate had an ironic twist in store for Tim Fisher's parents: one of their three children would turn out to be gay—and he would be the only one to give them grandchildren.

Even as a little boy, Tim knew he wanted to be a father: "I always had that strong drive."

The middle child, six years older than the younger of his two sisters, Tim remembers urging his parents in vain to have more children. So when at age twenty-one, he told his mother he was gay, she expressed sadness for him as well as for herself—because "you'll never be able to be a parent." Tim remembers:

"Without even having thought of it at the time, I told them I wasn't prepared to give that up yet. But it was back before gay parenting was even on the radar screen."

But he found the way. And since the birth of his two surrogate-born children, Tim has been a stay-at-home dad who proudly says he was "always the classroom party parent."

Tim and his partner Scott Davenport have been together for nearly thirty years, since they met as college freshmen. They now live in Bethesda, Maryland, in a home chosen for its proximity to a high school whose excellence is nationally recognized. Their daughter Kati entered her first year there in 2004, with brother Fritz set to follow two years later.

The children would appear to be treading a high-level academic path with sure-footed confidence. In eighth grade, for example, Kati displayed her comfort with the nature of her family by choosing "gay marriage" as her topic for presentation in a classroom debating unit.

The children's seemingly smooth course is an ongoing tribute to their fathers' resolute pilgrimage through the wilderness of gay male parenting in the 1990s.

Both Tim and Scott grew up in the Philadelphia area, Tim in a devoutly religious home, Scott in what he calls "a regular, go-to-church-on-Sunday kind of home." Tim's father was the principal, his mother head of the nursery school, at a Lutheran school. Scott was an only child and grew up in a house in which his parents still live, summering each year at a Methodist camp meeting where his father was on the board of directors. Tim and Scott became an item in 1976 shortly after both enrolled at the University of Pennsylvania. Their relationship became a long-distance one for two years after graduation, when Tim enrolled in a graduate anthropology program at the University of Arizona.

When Scott completed his five-year Bachelor's and MBA program at Penn's Wharton School, he signed on as a strategist with a Washington, D.C. consulting firm and was joined there by Tim, master's in hand, a year later. But Tim, not surprisingly, found anthropology to be "not the most marketable field in the word" and he drifted instead into direct marketing.

Tim had never lost what he calls his "burning interest" in becoming a parent and the two "talked about it off and on." But for some years, it didn't seem a realistic option. Tim monitored the gay press for some years during which he found a grand total of one story about a gay father—about a man who had had his child during an earlier marriage. As it would turn out, the men would actually have their first child before knowing any other gay male parents whatever. Tim says:

"We knew we weren't the first, but we did it in a vacuum of information and we feel like pioneers. We figured there had to be some out there, we just didn't know how to find them. There was no internet, no books. We just had to go it on our own when we thought the time was ripe for us."

Assuming they would need to adopt, but clueless as to how openly gay men should go about it, they placed an ad in the Washington gay newspaper, the *Blade*, seeking information from gay and lesbian parents. It elicited a single response—from a woman interested in becoming a surrogate mother.

For them, it was a wholly new idea. But they researched surrogacy, got to know the woman and—by now approaching what they considered the ripe old age of thirty—decided to stop talking and just do it. Tim provided the sperm, and fifteen months after they had placed the ad, Kati was born. When Kati was about one, they started planning for another child. The original surrogate was no longer available, having moved. But they were so pleased at how Kati's birth had gone that this time they advertised in the *Blade* specifically for a surrogate. And again, everything went well. When Kati was a little over two, she was joined by little brother Fritz.

Scott says he would initially have been content to live his life without children. But once they came, he now can't imagine otherwise. He compares himself with a lot of heterosexual men who don't necessarily look forward to parenthood but once children arrive become devoted parents: "I've enjoyed every minute of it."

A few years earlier, Tim had formed his own marketing consultancy firm, so he prepared for parenthood by simply refusing any new accounts and retaining only what he considered the most interesting. And by the time Fritz was born, he was already virtually a full-time dad.

But they were still having trouble finding other gay dads. As Tim remembers:

"It seemed we knew all the gay fathers in the country. And in fact we probably did know a significant proportion of them. If we found a gay couple with kids, we put them our Christmas card list. You could do that, there were that few of us."

In Washington, through their pediatrician's Dupont Circle practice in the heart of D.C.'s gay community, they found other same-sex, mostly lesbian, parents. With them, they formed toddler play groups they describe as "lifelines for us," and many of the other parents remain some of their closest friends today. But Scott was moving up the ladder in his firm, which opened a New York office and transferred him there shortly after Fritz's birth. So the family moved to Montclair, New Jersey, where Tim continued to prospect for families like theirs.

The pickings were so sparse that when Tim and Scott held picnics at their New Jersey home for gay dads and prospective dads, some would drive from as far as three states away to be there for the afternoon.

"They would tell us, 'Oh, you're the only gay fathers we've ever met.' Many of them were wannabes, and we were the only couple they could find. You can collect all the information you can find, but for many, they have to meet a real person who has actually done it, and then they can say, 'Okay, now!'"

It was while in Montclair that they teamed up with Wayne Steinman and Sal Iacullo to lead discussions of same-sex parents and wannabes, including what might have been the first group for men only.

Both Tim and Scott served with Wayne Steinman on the board of the Gay and Lesbian Parents Coalition International, and Tim was its unpaid volunteer executive director from 1993 to 1997. Now known as Family Pride Coalition with a Washington staff under Executive Director Aimee Gelnaw (see chapter 2), the organization is a sort of lifeline for thousands of families with gay and lesbian parents. Its premier event is its Family Week in Provincetown, Massachusetts, a sort of same-sex parenting Mecca to which hundreds of families each summer now make their annual pilgrimage.

And one Family Week highlight is the presentation of an annual award named for Tim and Scott: the Fisher-Davenport Award for Outstanding Contributions to Our Families, recognizing the massive assistance they've given to other families through the years.

For many of the families, who come from every part of America and some five other countries, the Province-town Family Week is the highlight of their year, and the Fisher-Davenport clan routinely also spends the week prior to Family Week in Provincetown.

In 1997, Scott joined the financial firm Capital One in its Washington office. But now with children of school age, he and Tim decided not to move back to the District of Columbia itself, but to the Maryland suburb of Bethesda and specifically just blocks from highly-rated Walt Whitman High School. Tim's assessment of their community:

"If there are homophobes here, they're the ones who have to stay in the closet."

He attributes that in large part to the fact that Bethesda is an affluent, well-educated community. But he perhaps underplays his and Scott's own role in assuring a comfortable environment for their kids.

During their years in New Jersey, Washington's

Rainbow Families had pretty much become defunct. So one of their first tasks on return was to revitalize it, thereby creating a broad social network for them and their children. Kati was starting second grade and Fritz was in kindergarten. But the elementary school welcomed parental help, and Tim was at school almost as much as the kids—working with small groups of children, reading to them, working with a student play, volunteering wherever needed. And he was often there at night, too, as an active member of the PTA.

It was at this point that Tim became "the classroom party parent," organizing the celebrations held occasionally at their home but more often at school for such events as Halloween, Christmas and Valentine's Day. And in any class his children were in, Mother's Day became Primary Caregiver's Day—"That's the day I got my card." As he says:

"If you're a little proactive and tell the teacher, in case they haven't thought about it, that you want your kid to do something different, they're usually open to that."

Well, anyway, that's the way it worked in Bethesda.

"It all helped me get to know the kids and their parents, and to introduce our family and its unusual nature to the school community."

For both Tim and Scott, doing workshops for younger gay dads soon became a major avocation. Typically, those who attend are a mix of "wannabes" and those with children of all ages who might or might not be encountering problems at their schools.

Now in their late forties, Tim and Scott find themselves surprised—and encouraged—by the youth of most of the men who attend. And some of them are single, such as those two at the workshop on the *Norwegian Dawn*.

"If you have that burning desire," Tim notes, "sometimes you're not going to wait for a partner. But I'm just amazed when I see a single dad with more than one child. They're the ones I take my hat off to."

At the workshops, they always stress the importance of being proactive in their children's schools and in joining groups of other same-sex parents. They think it's especially important for the children to attend such events as the Family Weeks sponsored by Family Pride. And on that point, the testimony of every youngster who has ever been there bears them out. (See, for example, the experience of Danielle Silber, chapter 7.)

At home, too, the dads' social life bolsters the children's positive image of nontraditional families. While Tim and Scott see a mix of gay and straight friends, with and without children, Tim says that, "We probably hang out with lesbian moms more than anyone else." And many of Kati's and Fritz's friends are children of lesbian mothers.

For some years, of the two dads, Tim was the primary workshop leader, but they now usually do them together. And Scott each year does one without Tim at American University. There, he's the gay dad on a diverse sociology class "Dad's Panel" that usually also includes a heterosexual stay-at-home father, a working father and at least one who is African American.

Tim recalls one incident that for him particularly underlines the importance of the children's familiarity with families like their own. It happened when Kati was five and Fritz was three and in nursery school. The kids were at the dining room table and Tim was in the kitchen preparing the next course, when he overheard Fritz tell his sister, "Joshua said I can't have two dads."

Joshua was Fritz's best friend and Tim and Scott were friendly with his parents and knew the parents had no problem with their family. Tim assumed that Joshua's statement was probably Joshua's inarticulate way of expressing his first realization that Fritz's family was different from his own. But Kati saved Tim the trouble of interceding.

"Kati told him, 'Oh, when someone says that, you say . . .,' and she went through the laundry list of all the different kinds of families she knew. Some 'have two moms like so-and-so,' some have 'two dads like so-and-so' and so on.

"Fritz was just nodding, and neither of them was the least bit upset, because we had been active, and they knew so many different families that they knew the rules weren't as clear-cut as some people might think they were.

"And that was very, very important to them."

As noted above, much of the kids' comfort owes to their annual stay at the Provincetown, Massachusetts Family Week, where they're in touch with scores of children with gay and lesbian parents. In 2004, their dads bought a second home in Provincetown, so that they can spend an extra week there each year prior to Family Week.

And, oh, yes: since Provincetown is in Massachusetts, their dads can get married!

Esera Tuaolo and Mitchell Wherley

In college at Oregon State University, Esera Tuaolo won the Morris Trophy as the top defensive lineman in the Pac-10, made honorable mention All-America, set school records for sacks and tackles, and was a second-round draft choice of the Green Bay Packers. In his first National Football League season, he made the NFL all-rookie team. In 1999, he played in Super Bowl XXXIII with the Atlanta Falcons.

But he was miserable all those years, he told a damp-eyed crowd listening to his story on the *Norwegian Dawn*. He lived in constant fear of being exposed as gay, in a macho culture where "I could lose everything if as much as a rumor got started." He was afraid even to use a cell phone to communicate with Mitchell, lest the call be overheard. On an occasion most players would consider an honor, when his life-size picture formed the background of a widely distributed publicity poster, he could feel only fear: What if it was seen by someone who knew of his secret life? Aside from Mitchell during those years, he said, "My friend was tequila." Thoughts of suicide were no stranger to him.

He recalled his muscles tightening after one loss when the coach berated the team, "You played like a bunch of fags!" But the fear converted into a secret chuckle as the coach added, "except for Tuaolo."

Except for the fact that he played in the NFL, he said, his story of his years in the closet contains the same elements of isolation, depression, and anxiety attacks as other closeted gay men. But those years of fear contained a silver lining. They helped him get started on his true life's ambition—a singing career in show business.

As a Green Bay rookie, he had to go through an initiation rite that required every rookie to stand and sing as a prerequisite to taking his place at the dinner table. He did what he describes as a "Gospel-tinged version" of "Mary Had a Little Lamb," and the spontaneous performance was so successful that a month later he became the first player ever to sing the national anthem at a nationally televised game. It would happen twice more during his career. He would also make a number of pop albums and videos during his football years.

He came out in 2001, shortly after his NFL retirement, in an interview with Bryant Gumbel on HBO's *Real Sports*. He did so, he says, because of his family. As he puts it on his Web site (www.eseratuaolo.com): "No more lies, no more pain, no more acting, just living in our truth. We want our children to know that their fathers are proud and comfortable with who they are."

The Gumbel interview prompted thousands of positive e-mail, and only a few negative, from around the world. But a San Francisco 49er running back, Garrison Hearst, would confirm Tuaolo's perception of most NFL players by telling the *Fresno Bee*, "I don't want any faggots on my team. I don't want any faggots in this locker room." (Tuaolo is proud, though, that he can count all-time Packer quarterback great Brett Favre among his personal friends from his football days.)

In January 2003, the organization PFLAG (Parents, Families and Friends of Lesbians and Gays) announced a national scholarship program for GLBT students and named one of the scholarships after Tuaolo. At a press conference in the National Press Club in Washington, D.C., Tuaolo was the featured speaker; he opened his appearance by quietly asking the audience to stand, then delivering a stirring a cappella rendition of the national anthem. One critic has described his robust falsetto-style voice as "gorgeous" and likened it to that of another big man, pop legend Aaron Neville.

Still, his remarks that day, as on the *Norwegian Dawn*, focused largely on his family life with Mitchell and their adopted twins, Mitchell, Jr. and Michelle. When he was envying his teammates with their wives, children, and suburban homes, he never thought the same was possible for him. But now, he says, "I have a spouse, two children, two dogs, and the picket fence in the suburbs."

4.

The Mayor and His Granddaughters: Three Generations of "Something Right"

W hen Tom Potter was Portland, Oregon's chief of police, a Portland *Oregonian* feature about his family won an in-house award as the "consummate story of parental acceptance." It quoted a local psychologist's blunt assessment: "Something right happened in that family."

In November of 2004, Potter was elected Portland's mayor. But because he had imposed a twenty-five dollar cap on campaign contributions—against an opponent with a million-dollar war chest—he was considered a sure loser when he gathered about thirty supporters for a campaign pre-launch dinner at Billy Reed's Restaurant in early 2004. At dessert time, he stood and started to explain his thoughts about the city's need for new leadership and vision.

As he spoke, two women rushed into the banquet room, breathlessly late, towing two little girls, one by hand, one in arms. They were Potter's daughter Katie and her life partner Pam Moen, the biological and adoptive mothers respectively of the two little girls, McKenzie, four and a half, and Madison, seven months. They had been necessarily delayed by "Kenzie's" very first school play, in which she played a monkey. Part of her costume, a paper cap on which she had painted her version of a monkey, was still stapled around her head.

Kenzie's brown eyes flashed with delight as she spotted her grandfather. Three times, but not loud enough for him to hear, she called out to him. Finally, patience at an end, she shouted more lustily, "Graan-paa!"

All eyes turned from the speaker to the adorable dark-haired girl, now dancing a jig of excitement. Tom grinned, his oratorical point lost for the moment, as he greeted her in return: "Hi, sweet girl." His audience broke into cheers and applause, captivated by Kenzie's bubbly charm.

"It was just so darn cute," Katie Potter recalls. "Here's this candidate trying to get his campaign going, and his little granddaughter is hollering at him because she wants to see him so badly. I had to keep her from running up there."

Katie and Pam are both Portland police officers, a couple for more than fifteen years, and their girls are the youngest of Tom's nine grandchildren born to his two sons and two daughters.

A few weeks later, television cameras rolling, Tom formally launched his mayoral campaign at a neighborhood clubhouse auditorium. His children and grandchildren all took the stage to introduce themselves, and Kenzie urged the crowd to "vote for my grandpa." Grandson Kyle, eleven, drew hearty applause when he announced, "I would vote for Grandpa if I could, but he'll have to wait until I'm eighteen." Discreetly tutored by Mom Pam, Kenzie also shouted during a momentary lull in the proceedings, to the delight of the audience, "Go, Tom, Go!"

In Grandfather's outspoken opinion—and he will admit to no bias—no two children "have ever grown up with more loving parents" than Kenzie and Madi. But he feels pretty much the same about the parents of his other grandchildren. It's a large and spirited extended family that rarely goes more than a few weeks without gathering for a noisy barbecue or a batch of Grandpa's special shrimp gumbo. And for some fifteen years, they've never missed a week-long summer clan campout at either the Oregon beach or mountains.

Kenzie and Madi are the latest of a long line of beneficiaries of that "consummate story of parental acceptance." But they are growing up, not merely in a caring and close-knit family, but in a metropolitan area whose cultural climate of openness traces in significant part to the powerful bond between their Mama Katie and Grandpa Tom.

Tom is generally acknowledged as probably the most

effective chief of police in Portland's history. As a national authority on community policing, he downplayed the long-run efficacy of arrests and lockup, assigning top priority to citizen-police partnership solving local problems together as a team. And just months after he became chief, when Katie came out publicly, the story of a proud and openly gay police officer, openly supported by an equally proud father who was also her chief, made national headlines.

Together, in the following years, they would play commanding roles in the cultural revolution that has shaped Portland into a city immune to many of the forces of sexual bias. In September of 2004, for example—amid a torrent of gay marriage bans sweeping the entire country—Portland's City Council unanimously approved a resolution favoring gay marriage and opposing the ban on that year's Oregon state ballot. A key speaker was Katie Potter, who told the Council that she and her daughters were not eligible for state survivor benefits paid to the spouses of officers killed in the line of duty.

"Of course, sudden death is the last thing on earth I want my family to experience. But . . . I would like to know that my family would be cared for, as any other police officer's family would be, if a line of duty death does occur."

As she spoke, Katie and Pam were one of nine couples, among three thousand gay pairs granted county licenses earlier that year, who were plaintiffs in a suit seeking to uphold those marriages. So their union was under attack in the court system as well as by the ballot measure before the Council that day. Despite losing by a wide margin in Portland itself, the ban would be approved by voters statewide a few months later. (See chapter 9.)

It was hardly the first time Officer Katie Potter had appeared before the Council as a successful advocate for gay families. Two years earlier, in a campaign she undertook shortly after McKenzie's birth, she had urged the Council to extend city disability and survivor benefits to domestic partners of gay police officers and firefighters. In the end then, too, there were no dissenting votes when the Council responded to her plea, "Please tell our daughter that her parents are as deserving as other families in Portland."

It was Katie's affection and respect for her father that first led her—at age five—to think about becoming a cop: "I had these dreams about a father-daughter team on the street, in a squad car. I still think it would be neat." The fantasy of course was not to be: long before Katie reached the police academy, her father was moving up the Police Bureau ladder and away from the street.

Inevitably, when they are older, her children will come to appreciate the debt their well- being owes to the police careers of Mama Katie and Grandpa Tom.

⁓

In her excellent book, *Families Like Mine* (see chapter 5), Abigail Garner lists some of the shared values that taken as a whole comprise what we mean when we refer to a "gay culture" or "queer culture." In the "Entertainment" category, for example, she lists the musical *A Chorus Line* and "Drag shows and other campy entertainment." Under "Food," she refers to "Appreciation of gourmet food" and "Swapping detailed stories of memorable meals."

And under "Values" is the item "Distrust in law enforcement."

Indeed, the event most often cited as giving rise to the very concept of a gay movement is a police raid of a Greenwich Village gay bar, the Stonewall Inn, which triggered the so-called Stonewall Rebellion of 1969. And even today, "macho" homophobic attitudes remain common in the field of policing, perhaps second in degree only to professional sports. While attitudes are slowly changing, police officers still all too often share an "Us versus Them" mentality in which "Us" allows little room for homosexuality.

It's one of the factors that gives special meaning to the story of Kenzie's and Madi's grandfather and mother.

When Tom Potter was a young patrol officer, the "Us versus Them" mindset was best reflected by the popular TV show *Dragnet*. The mantra of the fictional Sgt. Joe Friday—"Just the facts, Ma'am"—was the accepted credo, and it meant, "What we do as police is our business, and none of yours." Tom's career would turn on the starkly different philosophy that "Your business *is* our business"—that the top priority of the police should be to discover and promote the needs of each of society's different communities. And for him, that quite specifically included the gay and lesbian community.

Soon, Tom was preaching to a largely converted choir.

Residents generally cheered his reforms, including his emphasis on hiring more women and ethnic minorities. Still, many citizens—and perhaps most of his own officers—were dismayed when he extended his open door policy to gays and lesbians. For many, that was just a little bit too much community.

Tom met regularly with gay and lesbian leaders and openly recruited officers from within their ranks, even appearing personally on a local gay television show. He kept a rainbow-striped flag, a gift from the gay community, in his office. He stated publicly, "Some of the nicest people in this city are gays and lesbians." He testified before the state legislature in favor of a gay civil rights bill. Earlier, he had been perhaps the country's first police captain to march in uniform in a gay pride parade. Now he did so as chief—angering not only many on the religious right but also a number of his own officers.

As fortune would have it, his innovations within the bureau happened to coincide with the rise of a strident statewide antigay movement led by an organization known as the Oregon Citizens Alliance. As Tom was taking over as chief, the OCA launched a petition drive that would culminate in cultural warfare across the state over its far-reaching antigay proposal known as Measure Number Nine. (See chapter 1.)

Into this already volatile mix one more explosive ingredient was added—the public "coming out" of a lesbian police officer and her chief of police father.

⤙

Katie, slim and graceful with brown hair and lively brown eyes, bears a striking resemblance to her father in his own youth. But their bond plainly goes beyond external similarities. They also share an air of candor, warmth, humor, and inner peace. Their fondness and respect for each other appear boundless.

Katie was the third-born of Tom's four children. In her growing-up years, much of the future police officer's energy had gone into another type of policing— repressing her unbidden inner attractions to other girls and women. "I don't want to feel this," she told herself again and again. A natural athlete, she won a softball scholarship to Taft College. There, though still not out to her family, she came out to a few friends. The revelation brought a certain relief. But the other side of the coin was the taunting of some classmates, whom she remembers walking behind her and chanting in time with her footsteps, "Dyke, dyke, dyke."

Katie left college early to join the police bureau, where she was out to her fully supportive father and to a few friends, and where she assumed her lesbianism was common knowledge. And there, she met and fell in love with Pam Moen.

Pam was already an eight-year veteran when she was assigned to "cover" (remain on supervisory call) for Katie's first night as the sole officer in a patrol car. A native of the Portland area, Pam had taught physical education, health, and math in a Portland middle school for four years when an officer assigned to lecture there encouraged her to think about policing as a career.

"I had never considered it," she says. "But he got me

to thinking about it. Now, I tell people I figured that as long as I was already having to put up with so much discipline in the schools, I might as well carry a gun."

Her most harrowing experience on patrol occurred one night when she responded to two consecutive calls from a trailer park resident reporting intruders around his car and trailer.

She could find nothing awry and, alerted by the man's somewhat strange behavior, suspected he might be hallucinating. Sure enough, while surveilling the surrounding grounds and finding nothing amiss, she heard apparent gunshots from inside his trailer. She called for additional cars, and she and another officer approached the trailer, partially covered behind a hedge, while a dispatcher tried to talk the man into leaving the trailer. He finally did, but only after firing three rounds that missed Pam's head by no more than three feet. Then he leapt out of a window "like Rambo," Pam says, brandishing a rifle, ammunition belts strapped around his chest. And before he could be subdued, one of his shots found a target, killing a police canine that had leapt out of a partially open window of one of the patrol cars. Diagnosed as mentally ill, the man was committed to a state mental hospital.

By 1993, eleven years of such daily encounters with human frailties had given Pam what she calls "a short fuse"—a diminished sense of patience that she genuinely feared could, given the proper set of strained circumstances, cause her to needlessly hurt another person. She applied for a desk job opening but was turned down when the interviewing officer decided she belonged somewhere else—namely, in a recently rejuvenated Family Services Unit designed to reduce domestic violence. And there, she now continues to serve.

Her job, in effect, is to find and arrest perpetrators of domestic violence. Often, the first step is to break down the reluctance to press charges on the part of a victimized spouse or the parent of victimized children. But it is of course the arrest itself—by definition of a perpetrator capable of violence—that carries with it the ever-present potential of danger. Fortunately for her, and for Katie and their daughters—she remains so far unscathed.

Katie transferred to safer desk duty when Kenzie was born. But she recalls her patrol duty with fondness. Her most satisfying memories are those that evoked citizens' appreciation. She recalls one incident, for example, when a high-speed chase resulted in the capture of a young man who had brutally attacked his seventy-one-year-old aunt. It isn't the derring-do of the arrest that stands out in her mind. It's the appreciation she received when she returned to interview the attacker's aunt, whom she knew personally:

"She gave me a big smile and said, 'Oh, I'm so glad it's you.' I could see the comfort it brought her that it was me who came through the door and not some unknown in a blue uniform. It made me feel good to be a cop."

Another memorable incident involved her arrest of a woman drug addict, the mother of several children who were immediately removed to protective custody. As Katie drove the woman to jail, she talked to her, as was her custom in such cases, about the risks of drugs not only to herself but perhaps more importantly to her children.

"I remember talking about her little kids, how they could get hold of some of her drugs, think it's candy, overdose and die. And I told her about a relative of my own in a similar situation who was in danger of losing her children. I said, 'You can turn this thing around, but something has to be stronger than the addiction—for some, it's faith, or for others, love of your children. Whatever works.'"

The woman later sought out Katie to thank her and tell her that she was going to change so she could get her kids back. Katie recalls, "I was pleased, but you never know. More often than not, those pledges don't work out. But about a year later, she sent me a letter saying her life *had* changed and that she was close to getting her kids back. She had dumped all the people she had been running with, and she was taking classes, working toward something positive.

"It was an affirmation that what had happened to her the night of the arrest was important and had stayed with her. It's an example of why I want to keep doing police work."

Tom had always told Katie not to be deterred from coming out by concerns for his career. So a few months after he became chief, when a writer for a local gay publication suggested doing a feature story about her and her father, she and Tom concurred. The resulting cover story, with front-page pictures of the smiling father-and-daughter team, drew media attention across the country. It was 1990, and the story of an openly gay police officer openly supported by a father who was also her chief then added up to a front-page nugget.

Katie had built up a network of close officer friends, but now others turned hostile. Rumors circulated that she was having sex with young girls. Someone vandalized her personal car when she parked it in the police parking lot during a Pride parade, and she suspected other officers to be the perpetrators. She was the butt of subtle but pointed insults: the officer who handed out keys and radios for her shift sometimes ignored her, forcing her to walk around the counter to gather her own equipment.

"I don't think I'd still be in the bureau if it wasn't for Dad's support," she says. "He gave me the understanding and strength to keep going, assuring me that we did the right thing."

To the Oregon Citizens Alliance—already at odds with a police chief who marched in the Pride parade and actively recruited gays and lesbians for police work—Tom's open support of his lesbian daughter was definitely *not* "the right thing." Touting "traditional family values," the OCA held press conferences to denounce Tom and called for his removal.

By now, however, Tom's commitment to equality had won him important backing from city and state leaders. An *Oregonian* headline in mid-1991—"Groups Declare Support for Embattled Chief"—summed up the reaction of city and state leaders. The accompanying story quoted the head of the crime commission of the chamber of commerce as saying, "We are in complete agreement with the chief in accepting and allowing diversity." Governor Barbara Roberts issued a statement backing Tom's stand for diversity and privacy and against discrimination.

Nevertheless, the heaviest storms were yet to come, after the OCA succeeded in winning a place on the 1992 ballot for the draconian Measure Nine, which would have amended the state constitution, among its other far-reaching provisions, to equate homosexuality with pedophilia, sadism, and masochism. It touched off a vicious campaign throughout the state, and antigay animosity was the apparent cause of two deaths in Salem. (See chapter 1.)

In Portland, among other acts of mayhem, vandals burglarized the "No on Nine" office and destroyed its mailing list. Tom assigned special units to minimize violence from either side. His efforts to calm the situation failed to stave off death threats and further calls for his resignation.

Katie, ever the professional, says the most difficult aspect of the era for her was the need while on duty to soft-pedal her personal views when citizens, as they often did, voiced strong antigay sentiments. And she was keenly aware that she and her father were special targets of hostile fire from the right owing to their role in the media spotlight. For the first time, at Tom's suggestion, Katie began carrying her gun even while off duty.

"Normally, I just don't like to run around off duty with my gun," she says. "But he advised me to think about being armed wherever I go. So I knew it was pretty serious."

Pam, while publicly out and identified as Katie's partner in various newspaper stories, had not, like Katie, been the direct focus of media attention. So she did not feel herself at any particular increased risk. But it was a tense time for the entire gay community. "We all felt very attacked in an unfair way," she says.

On election day, rural counties approved the hate-filled measure by resounding margins that ran as high as two to one. But overwhelming disapproval in Portland defeated the measure statewide by the comfortable margin of 57 to 43 percent.

In the end, most citizens appreciated Tom's reshaping of the Police Bureau. As chief, the *Oregonian* wrote, Tom "put in place a style of policing that emphasizes conversation and problem-solving in place of handcuffs and revolving jail doors." When he retired, the newspaper editorialized that in just three years he had "brought the bureau closer to the citizens than any chief in contemporary times."

Oregonian columnist Steve Duin wrote about Tom and Katie as a team. "Over the years," he said, "they have added a few pages to the book on family values. They have helped to mend the once-troubled relationship between the Portland cops and the city's gay and lesbian community, patching up the differences from the inside."

It's hard for a casual observer not to be struck by how little Tom, Katie, and Pam fit the stereotypes of cops. To hear them talk, you might assume they were in social work or some other type of ministry to the needy, oppressed, and mistreated. And in fact they all say they chose their calling largely out of a desire to help others.

"That's what it's all about—helping other people and feeling good about what you've done at the end of the day," Tom says of his years in policing, and Katie and Pam nod.

~

At Potter family gatherings, Katie and Pam had always been favorite aunts, all the more beloved because of their exciting status as cops. But by the mid-1990s, a bevy of nieces and nephews had become insufficient. They wanted children of their own. So they joined a group of seven lesbian couples, all then childless but wanting to become parents.

Katie in fact was already pregnant, as was one of the other women. But Katie's first pregnancy resulted in a miscarriage, and by the time Kenzie came along in 1999, Katie and Pam were already laggards. Within the group, five girls and one boy preceded Kenzie—all born in just an eight-month span ending in July of 1999! And in February of 2003, with Madi's birth, Katie and Pam became the group's fourth couple with two children— although in two instances, the second child is a Guatemalan adoptee. Originally known as their "maybe baby group," it's become simply a full-fledged baby group with frequent noisy reunions rotating among members' homes.

Many lesbian couples choose a male friend as donor.

But none of this particular group chose that route, opting instead for agency donors.

Kenzie and Madi are full biological sisters, born to Katie via insemination by the same donor and legally adopted by Pam under Oregon's "second-parent adoption" provisions. Although the donor is anonymous, Katie and Pam in a sense feel they know him intimately, by way of a lengthy, minutely detailed agency profile of his vital statistics and personal characteristics. And, because he is what is known as an "identity release donor," Kenzie and Madi, each at age eighteen, will have the option of meeting him personally.

Unlike Katie as a child, Kenzie shows not the slightest tendency to become a tomboy. She loves ballet, frilly dresses, fingernail polish, long hair, and what Katie calls "all the princesses in the Disney videos." To Katie and Pam, that's proof positive of the overriding influence of biology over environment as factors in personal identity. Neither of them owns a single dress. Both have always shunned the typical feminine accessories such as skirts, fingernail polish, and makeup. But Kenzie provides a stark contrast in this regard.

"Someone said to me, 'That must be hard for you,'" Katie says. "I told them it's not at all hard to encourage Kenzie to be who she is.

"So we've put her in ballet class, painted her room pink, put all her princess stuff up everywhere, and she's perfectly happy."

Her preschool teacher echoes the point: "Kenzie likes to dress up. She's a real princess, with a dramatic flair."

Presumably, it's just a matter of a year or two before her equally beguiling and energetic little sister provides

some spirited competition in the drama department. But it's still too early to predict whether Madi will opt for the role of princess or tomboy—or something in between.

Katie and Pam seriously considered the male friend donor route. "We even had married heterosexual friends with kids of their own offer to be the donor," Katie says. "But in the end we thought about the law of unintended consequences—how relationships can change, and the kind of conflicts that could arise down the road. So we decided we didn't want anyone else to share any of the responsibility. And we have plenty of male role models already in our family."

"With an identity release donor, we feel we get it all," Pam explains. "The kids will get to know who he is. Meanwhile, we're free of potential complications." Otherwise, they imagined, a donor might someday decide he wanted some sort of custody rights. Or the donor—or for that matter, a parent of the donor with no other grandchildren —might demand visitation rights beyond what the mothers felt reasonable and helpful.

"We wanted things cleaner," says Katie. "It's easier for us to know that we are the only two who can make decisions about such things as education and discipline and where we will live. All of those things can be up for grabs when other people become involved."

It's a very personal decision, the women believe, one that only each couple themselves can decide.

"Any way that works so that children have parents who love them, that's terrific," Katie says. "We just knew that for us, we wanted to be the primary parents and didn't want to be making decisions with other people."

Kenzie and Madi of course are thankfully still unaware of the condemnation pouring over their family from religious leaders, politicians, the Vatican, radio talk shows, and perhaps a majority of their fellow Americans. But shortly after she learned to speak, Kenzie looked around at her cousins, aunts and uncles and grandparents, and asked the inevitable question: "Why don't I have a father?"

There are many different kinds of families, she was told, and some have two fathers or two mothers. One of Kenzie's favorite television shows at the time happened to be *The Little Mermaid*, which gave her mothers the opportunity to point out that its principal character, Ariel, has no mothers and just one father. And their baby group provides routine examples of families similar to hers. "The girls get to see that there are lots of families out there just like their own," Katie says. "They get to see it, to sense it, to hear the other children and what they call their mommies."

Her mothers also took the opportunity—the first installment of what they foresee as an evolving explanation—to introduce Kenzie to the term "donor."

"Of course she had no idea of what a donor is, but we wanted her to get used to the term," says Katie. "Her peers are going to ask, 'Do you have a father,' and she can say, 'No, I have a donor.' As she gets older, she'll understand more about what it means—we'll tell her a donor is someone who gave us something, called sperm, that we needed for me to get pregnant. We'll explain that to make a baby you need sperm and an egg, and that men have sperm and women have eggs.

"We can tell her something like, 'Since you have two mommies, we don't have any sperm and the donor gave us the sperm so we could have you.'"

They have even considered eventually celebrating the donor's contribution on Father's Day, but referring to it as Donor's Day, marked by some special observance because, as they have already explained to Kenzie, "We appreciate what he has done to help us create our family."

They have kept his file from the agency, in case the girls some day want to know why they chose him: "They'll be welcome to go through it any time they want," Katie explains. "We'll sit down with them and go over it with them and answer any questions they might have."

The women have no illusions about what is in store for them. "As a same-sex couple, you shouldn't have kids unless you're prepared to deal with all the issues that are going to arise," Katie sums up.

Aside from the ongoing matter of getting neighbors accustomed to the atypical family makeup (discussed below) the issues begin as early as preschool. At Kenzie's first school, where she was the first enrollee with same-sex parents, the registration forms asked for the names of the "mother" and the "father" until, at her mothers' urging, they were changed to ask simply for the names of "parents." But the school continued to hold separate "Mom's Night" and "Dad's Night." (Katie enlisted her father to take Kenzie on the latter occasion, but thinks a general "Parent's Night," welcoming either parent, might work better.) Mother's Day was no problem: when the children were asked to draw flowers for their mothers, Kenzie simply drew two instead of one. For Father's Day, Kenzie honored her grandfathers, but the occasion started Katie and Pam thinking about celebrating "Donor's Day."

In all, as the school's pioneer lesbian mothers, while a few parents went out of their way to welcome Katie and Pam, they still felt something like outsiders. So for Kenzie's second year of preschool, they found a more congenial one where there were other same-sex parents and diversity is woven securely into the curriculum. There also, Katie makes a special point of being active in school affairs and making contact with other mothers.

"At first," she says, "I was often asked, 'What does your husband do?' And I'm quick to respond, 'I have a female partner and we have two children; she works full-time, I'm the stay-at-home mom right now.'"

To be more precisely accurate, except for her maternity leaves immediately following the birth of each girl, Katie is sort of a stay-at-home-as-much-as-possible mom. She's cut back to part-time duty, three days a week And Pam has rearranged her work schedule to coordinate with Katie's, so that they need a sitter only for part of two days a week to care for Madi at home.

"A couple of families at school immediately went out of their way to make us feel comfortable, and I went out *my* way to connect with others so that Kenzie could more easily make friends with their kids, which she has. But no matter what we do, we still feel different, like any other minority."

Still, after Katie and Pam were formally married on

March 3, 2004 (see below), and brought Kenzie to school the day after the wedding ceremony, "Everyone gave them a big hug," says a teacher there.

The same teacher says, "When I think of McKenzie, I think of her eyes always bright and always being so excited to do whatever the next thing is. She's just so engaging, and she always wants to tell a story. Maybe about what she did over the weekend, or just anything."

⁓

When she went off patrol duty in 1999 in deference to impending motherhood, Katie was assigned to a series of desk jobs, one of them as liaison officer to the Portland Fire and Police Disability and Retirement Fund. There, she dealt with officers' issues about retirement, injuries, illness, disability, and leave. And it became glaringly apparent to her how unprotected her own family was.

In the event one of them was killed in the line of duty, Katie realized, "We weren't going to get that call saying here's your survivor benefit. We could lose our partner, our home, our ability to support our children—all of those things that are in place as long as you're married. But of course we couldn't fix the problem by getting married."

Thus began a prolonged campaign to achieve equity for the estimated 5 percent of police and firefighters in committed same-sex relationships. She took her case first to the trustees of the Disability and Retirement Fund, then to Mayor Vera Katz, and finally to the media.

She encountered opposition at each step, particularly from the trustees, but ultimately convinced each in turn. (In the mayor's office, she received significant help from the mayor's openly gay chief of staff—current Councilman Sam Adams.)

On February 13, 2002, Katie argued for her plan before the City Council. Her voice catching in emotion, she pleaded, "Please tell our daughter that her parents are as deserving as other families in Portland."

Without a single dissenting vote, the Council did so, voting to amend the city charter to extend pension benefits to same-sex domestic partners of police officers and firefighters. "There's no doubt about it," said then-Mayor Katz. "It's the human thing to do."

At the same time, employing a bit of obvious logic that typically escapes most lawmakers in the country, the Council withheld the benefits from heterosexual domestic partners who, unlike their gay and lesbian counterparts, had the legal power to become married.

Five months later, Kenzie sat between her two mothers, Katie in uniform, in a horse-drawn stagecoach at the head of the annual gay pride parade, with Tom and his wife Karin Hansen marching alongside. Katie was the celebration's grand marshal, so honored for her dogged lobbying crusade to achieve equity for the same-sex partners of police and firefighters. And Kenzie's bright eyes popped wide as she laughed and waved in response to the massive cheers and applause from the gay men and lesbians lining the streets.

The *Oregonian* quoted an organizer of the event as saying, "Potter's choice as grand marshal was a natural."

All the members of the family campaigned actively for Tom during his successful 2004 run for mayor. But in fact, they were of two minds about his decision to return to public life. Son Troy probably spoke for all of them shortly after election when he said, "I think he'll be a great mayor. But as much time as we've all been able to spend together in recent years, I'm frankly jealous of the time the job will take."

Similarly, Katie and Pam lament the "good old days" when Kenzie and Madi spent time with their grandfather several times a week. Katie says Kenzie feels a "special tie" to Tom, and during his busy campaign, she was moved regularly to ask, "When do I get to see Grandpa again?"

One rainy day during the campaign, en route to Kenzie's school, Katie stopped at Tom's and ran to the front door to deliver a message. Kenzie, in her car seat, yelled, "Grandpa, I want to hug Grandpa." She got her hug, and Tom, hat- and coat-less, got drenched.

Before the run for office, Tom and Karin bicycled daily and stopped by often at Katie's and Pam's house. Sometimes they'd happen by while Katie, Pam, and the girls were having dinner and would join them for the meal. Other times, Kenzie spent the night with Tom and Karin. But Katie says, "Those days are gone and Kenzie's really feeling it. The connection is very important to her." In effect, as she and Pam see it, her family is sacrificing some of their own joys for the good of the city as a whole.

After retiring as chief, for eleven years Tom was

indeed available literally at a moment's notice to any of his family, including virtually daily visits with his mother until her death in a retirement home in 2002 at age ninety-six. And now, civic duties notwithstanding, the entire clan still gathers for every holiday and birthday, those regular barbecue and gumbo treats, and the annual week-long summer outing.

Kenzie's fourth birthday party, some months before Tom decided to run for mayor, was typical of the many gatherings. For the occasion, Katie and Pam transformed the backyard of their home in a normally quiet Southeast Portland neighborhood into a kind of one-ring circus ground. A jumbo rental tent emblazoned "Hoppity House" took up most of the yard, emitting joyful squeals from eight tots, all six or younger, leaping on its trampoline base. In the narrow ring of remaining space around the tent, some thirty adults and a dozen or so teenagers milled about, chatting and munching from plates piled with food from a diverse array on the kitchen table just inside.

All but a handful of the adults, and most of the teenagers, were part of Kenzie's extended family—grandparents, aunts, uncles, and cousins. Also on hand were a lesbian couple, Mick and Kat, longtime friends of Katie and Pam whom they affectionately call their daughters' "fairy godmothers."

The careers of many of the relatives reflect the extent to which the family has been involved in civic affairs and contributed more than its share to Portland's regular ranking as one of the country's most livable cities. Grandfather Tom won dozens of community, regional, and national awards for his pioneer advances in community policing. Tom's father-in-law, Herb Hansen, was for years considered the dean of Portland social workers as director of social services for the state's largest provider of children's services. His mother-in-law Joan Hansen, who is blind, is still active on a board responsible for the compliance of city buildings with the Americans with Disabilities Act. Tom's wife Karin Hansen taught for some years at Vocational Village, which works with disadvantaged children with serious emotional and behavioral problems. Tom's brother Dan spent twenty years with the Oregon Liquor Control Commission. Dan's wife Cindy once supervised all of the state's funeral homes as director of the Oregon State Mortuary Board.

Katie and Pam had bought this house and moved there from a distant part of the city just a few months before Madi's birth. It's a sunny, pleasant, and roomy place, but its primary attraction to the women, as mothers, was its location within a few blocks of the homes of grandparents Tom and Karin and of Katie's brother Troy, his wife Peggy, and their two children, Kyle and Kate.

Now, while others eat, Grandpa for a time has to forgo food and drink, his arms otherwise occupied cradling then five-month-old Madi as he talks with his brother Dan and Dan's wife Cindy. After a bit, he surrenders Madi to his ex-wife, Grandma Ginger, who is chatting with the girls' other grandparents, Pam's parents Fred and Vi Moen. In all, the gathering includes three of the girls' uncles, two aunts, nine cousins, and their step-grandmother Karin.

At their old house, where they had lived for ten years,

Katie and Pam were friendly with all the neighbors, and among those present today are three children and three adults from the old neighborhood, including the mother from next door there. Now, Katie tells a guest, they're still somewhat uneasy in the new location:

"We don't know whether there is someone in this neighborhood who is going to be offended by our family. We knew when we moved that at least for awhile we weren't going to be as comfortable here. It takes time to develop those sorts of relationships.

"But, for the girls' sake, it's important to be closer to Dad and the others."

By the time of Kenzie's fifth birthday the following year, they had made friends with many of the neighbors. And the party that year had to be split into two sessions: one, from 1:30–3:30 PM for some twenty-plus of Kenzie's preschool friends, and the second, from 4–6 PM, for the family itself. The Hoppity House once again was in place—but with an increased noise level in proportion to the swollen number of hoppers.

A few weeks later, the clan gathered for their annual campout at a beach campground near Manzanita, Oregon. Katie and Pam parked their twenty-two-foot house trailer, in which they've been camping for years, on a site near Troy and Peggy's spacious pop-up trailer and not far from the venerable VW Westphalia camper of Tom and Karin. Other family members—Kim and three of her children, Kevin and his son Jordan—raised tents on nearby campsites. They were joined by Pam's brother, sister-in-law, and niece, and by Karin's sister, brother-in-law, and their two young children, among others.

The youngsters spent long hours on the beach, fishing for salmon with Troy, riding along the beach with some of the parents on fifteen horses (a special treat courtesy each year of Grandpa Tom), and taking lessons from Tom and Karin on the intricacies of maintaining their balance on a recumbent bicycle. (During the retirement years, Tom and Karin traversed Portland's bike trails several times a week on recumbent bikes; for the mayoral campaign, a local biking club produced a T-shirt bearing Tom's picture on his bike together with the message, "Vote for the recumbent, not the incumbent.") Family friends dropped in from Portland to spend a day and join the family circle for the nightly barbecue.

It's a happy clan, and typically none is happier than Kenzie, a prancing child of boundless vigor, precocious self-assurance, and a sunny disposition marked by a hair-trigger impish grin. A few weeks after the beach outing, she entered her second year at her preschool, where a teacher says that of all the pupils there, "No one is more enthusiastic than Kenzie." But she plainly needs to ready herself for sibling competition from Madi, who by age one and a half was already displaying an assertiveness and perpetual-motion energy that had her mothers shaking their heads in weary admiration.

⁓

With a city population of under 600,000, and a metropolitan area numbering about 1.5 million, Portland is dwarfed in size by the major metropolitan areas—New York, San Francisco, Los Angeles, Chicago—that are

generally thought of as the nation's gay meccas. But
thanks in large part to a series of progressive civic
leaders like Tom Potter over the past few decades—and
despite massive conservative blocs in the state's rural
areas—Portland's welcoming vibes now make it one of
the nation's most gay-friendly cities.

When gay marriage became legal in Canada, Ted
Fettig and Kregg Arntson of Portland were among the
first to be wed in Vancouver, British Columbia.
Shortly thereafter, a married couple sent out party
invitations that read: "Karla Wenzel and Fred Miller
invite you to a special reception in honor of the marriage of Ted Fettig and Kregg Arnston. Join us as we
celebrate Ted making an honest man of Kregg (or is it
the other way around?)."

Karla Wenzel is a former chair of Portland's school
board. Until his retirement, Fred Miller was executive
vice president of city's largest utility, Portland General
Electric. The Portland *Oregonian*, in reporting the story
of the reception, cited it as evidence of a cultural fact:
"In Portland, relationships between gays and straight
people move with an ease and fluidity unlike many other
cities in the nation."

Being openly gay, for example, is no hindrance to
public office. In 2004, voters elected openly gay Sam
Adams to the City Council, and his campaign Web site
included a picture of him arm-in-arm with his domestic
partner. In the same election campaign, Tom's opponent
for mayor, Jim Francesconi, announced in favor of gay
marriage. And Francesconi did so despite the fact that at
one point he had said he said he was personally

opposed—thereby demonstrating his apparent belief that an antimarriage stance was simply not politically viable in Portland.

The proof of that particular pudding had jelled earlier that year when gay marriage blossomed as a national issue. San Francisco and Massachusetts cornered the national media spotlight market in that regard, but in fact the number of such unions reported in Portland (3,022) was not markedly fewer than those in San Francisco (3,955)—and far greater, as a proportion of its metropolitan area population, which is perhaps one-quarter that of the San Francisco Bay Area.

On March 2, 2004, on the strength of a legal opinion that Oregon's statute limiting marriage to one man and one woman violated the state constitution, Multnomah County commissioners ordered clerks to issue marriage licenses to same-sex couples. The next day, Katie Potter and Pam Moen were among hundreds of couples married in the downtown Keller Auditorium. Katie's father Tom cancelled scheduled mayoral campaign appearances and with his wife Karin stood in the rain with the women for two hours in a blocks-long line of couples, their friends and loved ones, waiting for admittance to the auditorium.

Inside, they were joined by family members, their daughters' godmothers Mick and Kat, and a group of family friends, one of whom had brought Kenzie and Madi. Typical of weddings everywhere, tears flowed generously as a volunteer minister announced, "By the authority vested in me by the State of Oregon, I pronounce you married."

Some evenings later, Katie and Pam were admiring their decorative marriage license, lying on a living room table, when McKenzie grabbed a pen and had scribbled the first two letters of her name, "MC." Her mothers stopped her from writing further, telling her, "That's a special piece of paper." But Kenzie saw other signatures and asked whose *they* were. "We pointed out the officials' signatures," Katie says, and told her, 'Great Godmother Kat signed here, and this is Mama and Mom's signatures here.' And she was so sad and she said, 'Well, no one will know that I was there.'"

Touched, Katie and Pam talked about it after putting Kenzie to bed and decided that because it was important to her, Kenzie should be allowed to sign it, which she did the next morning.

"She was so delighted," Pam says. "It made her day to be able to write her name—big letters, little letters— right across the middle of that certificate."

But of course, the ultimate legality of their marriage was another, still undecided question. Within a month Katie and Pam had joined nine other same-sex couples as plaintiffs in an action brought by the American Civil Liberties Union to test the validity of the Oregon statute limiting marriage to one man and one woman. The others included two librarians, two doctors, a law professor, a fitness trainer, a musician, and a stay-at-home mother.

The legal complaint pointed out that Pam's duties bring her "into contact with potentially violent situations" and listed the state benefits available to surviving spouses, but not domestic partners, of officers killed in the line of duty. (They include an immediate $25,000 death benefit, plus other health, education, and mortgage payments.)

Shortly thereafter, a petition by anti-gay-marriage forces succeeded in placing an amendment on the state constitution, approved statewide the following November, limiting marriage to one man and one woman. At a subsequent press conference with other litigants in the court action, Kenzie and Madi were at their mothers' side. There, a television reporter asked Kenzie what she thought about the amendment and was noticeably astonished by the vehemence of the little girl's response:

"I think a woman should be able to marry another woman, and a man should be able to marry another man." Her eyes flashed even more brightly than usual as she emphatically added:

"It's just *not fair!*"

> "They even give cockroaches the rank of family now because they live under the same roof. If there's a cat, a dog, two lesbians and everything living there, it's a family."
>
> —*Cardinal Javier Lozsano Barragan, Vatican*

5.

Cherry-Picking the Truth: Children Protect Their Gay Parents

For parents on the R Family Cruise (see chapter 2), one highlight came on the next-to-last day at sea, when a panel of teenagers discussed growing up with gay and lesbian parents. Their comments were uniformly positive: "Growing up with two dads is awesome. I love it." "My family is as good as anyone else's." "We have a normal life. We do normal things." "Growing up in a gay household was easy." "My mothers are great." "They've been amazing parents."

The cheery portrayals of their family life were

undoubtedly sincere—but only part of a larger, more complicated picture that includes some harsh realities.

Among those in the audience was Abigail Garner, herself an adult child of gay parents and author of the acclaimed book, *Families Like Mine*. Afterward, parents typically told her, "Oh, that was so great. They were so brave to get up there and speak the truth." As Garner told me in a subsequent telephone conversation:

"And I'm thinking, 'Honey, that was not the truth. It was cherry-picking the truth.'"

Garner's on-board book readings revealed a far more complex version of reality. Cherry-picking aside, her book lives up to its subtitle—*Children of Gay Parents Tell It Like It Is*—by offering a look at the nuances, the woes as well as the joys, of life with same-sex parents.

Garner is a slender, attractive, articulate, woman in her early-thirties with long brown hair—and two gay dads and a heterosexual mother. She describes herself as "heterosexual but culturally queer," most at home in the gay culture.

Earlier that day, she had gone ashore in Nassau, where protesters greeted the *Dawn*'s arrival by demonstrating against gay marriage. Garner in turn greeted them wearing her trademark T-shirt bearing the message: "Some of My Best Parents Are Gay."

She founded and runs a popular Web site, www.FamiliesLikeMine.com, and has won numerous awards for her magazine and newspaper writing on the subject.

Garner is, in short, perhaps the reigning expert on what it's like to grow up with gay parents. She has devoted much of her adult professional life to assisting others to cope with the hardships she encountered. And for many, she says, one of the toughest parts can be protecting their parents from knowing many of the details of what society puts their children through.

Her own early years, unknown to any of her parents, were lived in fear.

To an outside observer, Garner's childhood would have seemed a model of middle-class normality. Her mother and father divorced about the time she started elementary school, but they lived close to each other in the same Minneapolis school district and gave priority to the well-being of her and her brothers. The arrangement worked so well that Abigail grew up with no idea of the concept of custody.

"I was really blessed that way," she says. "The unconventional divorce had an unconventional way of dealing with custody. So if my mom had a meeting, I was at my dad's house. If my dad was on a business trip, I was at my mom's house. After school, if I took the B Bus, I'm going to mom's house. If I took the E bus, I'm going to my dad's."

But the parents' split had come because her father was gay, and he then lived with his male partner. At school and elsewhere, she regularly heard comments degrading gay people and assuming that their children would necessarily be messed up if not outright abused: gay people were "deviants" and sought to "corrupt" children. So while she had no doubts about her own father's "normality," she had no way of knowing that he and his partner weren't exceptions to a general rule. Hence her worst fear:

"I thought every day that someone was going to take me away because gay people weren't supposed to raise children. So every time the doorbell rang, I thought I was going to be taken away."

It didn't matter whether she was at her father's or her mother's: "My fear of being taken away from my father was as real if I was playing in my mom's yard as if I were playing my dad's yard. A knock on mother's door would be the same thing as a knock on my dad's door."

Then she heard about a Minneapolis family with a gay father whose garbage cans had been set on fire. So now she had an added concern: "I was sure I was either going to die from arson or be taken away from my family."

By the time she reached high school, the fear of being "taken away" had dissipated. But she remained fearful of talking about her family. Her reluctance stemmed not so much from shame, she says, as from the fear of what exposure might wreak on her family. Gay people are sometimes killed just because they're gay: "We see examples all the time."

So she kept mum about her family except with a cadre of close friends and special teachers. This produced an amusing incident in her last year at a gathering of students, parents, and teachers, when a teacher who was unaware of her family situation praised her parents for providing the support she needed to do well—unlike "children who come from broken homes." The three of them, she writes in her book, had a good laugh about "passing as a white-picket-fence family."

It wasn't until she got to college, half a continent away from Minneapolis, that she felt safe talking about her family without putting them in danger.

After college, she spotted an announcement about a group of children with same-sex parents and called to see about joining. She was told, "No, this is for children." That made no sense to her, since she would always, at any age, be the child of a gay father. She persisted and became a volunteer support group leader.

She immediately learned that society's progress toward equal rights for gays has had little effect on the difficulties faced by their children. What she heard from the teenagers echoed her own experiences. And when she facilitated a discussion between a group of teenagers and some new gay parents, she came to the insight that led to her "cherry-picking" comment.

"What I found was that what the kids were telling the parents at this group—and they didn't even know any of the parents in the audience—was really different from the reality they were sharing in their own group.

"That resonated with me. What I immediately recognized was the way we as children censor ourselves from the whole truth in telling our parents. We've learned what we're supposed to tell our parents and what they don't want to hear. . . . Our job is to protect our parents from the toughest part of our childhood growing up.

"Often we do such a good job that our parents believe us. Parents want to believe it so badly that they do."

As Garner explains in her book, ugly stereotypes will fade only when the mainstream sees enough real-life gay-parented families to realize they are, on the whole, no different from any other. That means of course that these families, too, struggle with such things as alcoholism, depression, domestic strife, interpersonal conflicts. But if your parents are gay, you probably won't want your peers or counselors to know about such matters, lest they write it off to your parents' homosexuality. You'll probably want to keep a low profile, and you'll be tempted to internalize the shame that society seeks to heap on your family.

At the same time, your family status can create ideological mountains out of otherwise mundane molehills. If you need help with a learning disability, you are no different than many of your peers, but it's only in your case that anyone would think to link it to your father's love life. If you're one of a dozen caught in a particular month skipping class, only in your case might school officials blame the truancy on your mother's lesbianism.

Those who go before the media as teenagers, as did Alex Tinker (see chapter 1) and Danielle Silber (see chapter 7), face additional pressures. They're the representatives, the public face, of millions of others. They're under heavy pressure to come across as *beyond* normal, to reflect perfection both in themselves and their parents. But as far as their parents are concerned, Garner wonders whether it is really natural "for *any* teenager to be the cheerleader for how cool their parents are."

Aren't all these pressures lessening as society becomes generally more accepting and open to homosexuality?

Not necessarily, as Garner sees it.

For one thing, much of the progress has yet to reach the classroom and playground level. "If I'm still hearing the word 'faggot' on the playground," she says, "it doesn't really mean anything to me as a child that domestic partnership benefits are recognized by Fortune 500 companies or by the city government."

Perhaps more importantly, each step forward for gay equality typically produces a backlash that can actually worsen the children's plight. There is perhaps no better example than the national furor caused by the Massachusetts Supreme Court's 2004 decision to legalize gay marriage in that state. Subsequent polls revealed that while heavy majorities opposed gay marriage, somewhere around half or more of all Americans nevertheless favored Vermont-style gay civil unions affording many of the same rights as marriage. This represented a vast forward leap in societal attitudes from only a few years earlier. It seemed a clear harbinger of a gay-friendlier future. But meanwhile, the backlash produced twelve state laws, in 2004 alone, outlawing gay marriage. And even more punishing to the children of same-sex couples was the accompanying torrent of hostile denunciations of their parents.

The specter of gay marriage triggered a sort of holier-than-thou Olympic Games, in which politicians, religious leaders, and talk show hosts vied in rhetorical broadsides of condemnation and doomsday scenarios.

The gold medal perhaps belongs to a researcher for the organization Focus on the Family. Children of gay parents, he said, are "more likely to, *among other things*, suffer abuse, perform poorly in school, suffer lower levels of mental and physical health and wind up in trouble with the law." [Emphasis is mine.] What "other things," one is left to wonder, might the would-be seer have omitted to mention?

Or perhaps the top prize belongs to the Vatican for its
formal July 2003 pronouncement in which it told millions of innocent children that:

- Having gay parents is interfering with their "normal
  development."
- Their parents are "evil," "intrinsically disordered,"
  guilty of "deviant behavior" and "doing violence" to
  the children.
- Their family is "harmful to the common good."

Among the scores of other denunciations, a Baptist
minister told the kids their parents are "an abomination
to God." The President of the Family Research Council
trashed their families as a "black plague." A Democratic
delegate to the Maryland legislature said he didn't want
to live next door to them "and have my children playing
with them."

The backlash in effect brought the kids a double
whammy. They not only listened to themselves and their
families being denounced from on high. They inevitably
suffered also from intensified antigay hostility among
their peers. When supposed authorities are publicly
declaring that same-sex parenting presents a clear and
present danger to society, it tells mainstream Americans
that it's okay, even spiritually sound, to express any
antigay feelings they might harbor. And their dining
table conversations sooner or later end up on the playground and in the classroom.

So for the children, Garner says, "I think we're
much too quick to sign off on the conclusion that

times have changed. There are consequences that come with those changes."

⁓

Winston Miller (not his real name) grew up in a small Midwestern town. He, too, questioned the generally glowing accounts of the teen panel members.

When he was in sixth grade, Winston was seriously abused by both classmates and teachers because he had lesbian mothers. Severely beaten by a bully who pounded his head on the ground, Winston was suspended for trying to fight back; as additional punishment, he was ordered to clean the school rooms after a Father's Day observance! At a case conference with his teachers and mothers, two of the teachers stalked out after peremptorily announcing that having lesbian mothers was his problem. Winston, bawling, became near-hysterical.

Winston, now fourteen, simply couldn't believe that the teens on the panel could have encountered so little trouble. "It's too good to be true," he told his mothers. "They must be lying."

Nor, until some months before the cruise, were his biological mother Sally and second parent Olivia aware of metropolitan area parents like Sal Iacullo and Tim Fisher (see chapter 3) who were able to significantly ease their kids' paths there. Then, seeing ads for the cruise, they learned also of the existence of the Family Pride Coalition (see chapter 2), and have since become active Pride members. (At the mothers' request, their names have also been changed here.)

On the cruise, Sally says, "We met a lot families from California and the East Coast, but not many from the Midwest and none from a town like ours," Sally says. Their family is indeed living testament to the potential brutality of small-town ignorance.

The cruise was the first large-gathering "gay thing" they had ever done. Sally and Olivia say it was a "wonderful experience" just to see all the happy families. And Winston was wide-eyed much of the time. Still, he couldn't bring himself to reach out to any of the other teenagers. "He's very shy," Olivia says. "He stuck with us all the time. And after the first few days he was ready to come home."

The mothers now feel guilty that they hadn't taken pains when he was younger to seek out such groups as Family Pride that arrange gatherings for their kind of family. But information seeps slowly into small towns such as theirs.

They had been together some years, for example, yearning for parenthood but not even aware it was possible until they saw a Phil Donahue television show in the mid-'80s about donor insemination. Even then, they had to have the procedure performed in a city hundreds of miles away because their local gynecologist refused to do it.

Regular churchgoers in earlier years, they now no longer attend because of their cold reception as lesbians there. So it's somewhat ironic that the only accepting teacher they've found was a priest at a Catholic school—who later came out as gay and left the church.

They've had to alternate their work schedules to see to

Winston's care. The cruise was a financial burden but they intend from now on to take advantage of Family Pride's summer family weeks, one of which is held annually in the Midwest at Saugatuck, Michigan.

Their extended families, imbued with the small-town mindset, have been of little help. Only Sally's mother was genuinely supportive and personally involved with Winston. But she died a few years ago, another of life's blows for the boy.

Sally and Olivia, intelligent and articulate, have both worked at jobs requiring verbal sophistication. But the educational level of those they have to deal with at Winston's school was perhaps best demonstrated at a recent Book Sale Night for its some 500 families.

"Two families attended," Olivia laments. "We were one of them."

───⌒───

On one of the *Norwegian Dawn*'s main decks, a colorful portrait display entitled "That's So Gay" adorned the walls of a principal passageway. The portraits were of some two dozen teenagers and young adult members of COLAGE (Children of Lesbians and Gays Everywhere). Their pictures were accompanied by comments about their lives with same-sex parents.

Much like the statements at the teen panel, the youths' words in the display uniformly praise their parents and tell of the love and respect within their families. "For anyone who lends an ear, I will proudly tell them everything about my family, how great we are . . ." "I think

LGBT families are more loving than regular families." "Having gay dads has made my life fun . . . they can make anybody laugh." "Love is love, so what's wrong with that?" "The best part of having LGBT parents is that I am loved by two amazing people who want to take care of me and love me." "We are a unique family and I am very proud of my moms. They brought me up well." "I wish that people understood that my family is just like theirs in that we love, care, protect, and respect each other."

But the display doesn't wholly ignore the stigma that has haunted their lives:

Marina, fifteen, says people "yell at us, throw rocks at us, and vandalize our house simply because we're different."

Rachel, sixteen, was outed by a teacher and subsequently "teased constantly for about five years and it was hard to make friends."

Kate, eighteen, was "put into a trash can by a few seniors who saw the rainbow stickers on the back of my mom's car."

Abby, sixteen, was ridiculed in a classroom for having lesbian mothers and became so withdrawn that "for more than a year afterward I had difficulty letting new people into my life because I was afraid that they would find out . . ."

Aaron, fourteen, worries about being outed, wondering whether his friends would "still be my friends or would they think of me differently?"

Whitney, seventeen, says, "It's been hard having my mom's family gradually stop talking to us since she came out because we had been so close in the earlier years."

Joe, fifteen, has a lesbian mother and a father who "is straight and homophobic." A football player, he also hears "a lot of homophobic names during practice and games."

Expanding on these themes is a 2004 COLAGE collection of essays, short memoirs and poems entitled *Focus on MY Family: A Queerspawn Anthology*. ("Queerspawn" is a term used by some COLAGE members for children of same-sex parents.) It sketches the broad range of emotions sparked by the clash between their love of their families and the pain inflicted by society's prejudice.

A revealing essay by high school graduate Abigail Lawton goes to the core of why it is often difficult for children to be fully honest with their gay parents. She sums up the paradox that tortures so many young people (it "ate me up inside for years"): "I loved my moms, but I was ashamed of their relationship." Just walking down the street with them, she felt as though "every person we passed knew our secret and hated us for it." She imagined that "all eyes were on us, judging."

Until recently, she was baffled by her reaction since she firmly believed there is nothing wrong with love between two women or two men. "How can I feel this way?" she wondered.

"It took me a long time to realize what was right in front of my face, and an equally long time to accept it. The answer was that even though I truly believed that homosexuality was just as valid and natural as hetero-sexuality, I was living in a society that didn't. . . . Over the years, I had heard and seen enough to make me feel ashamed of my family, even though I knew there was nothing wrong with it."

Another pamphlet contribution, by Kelly Muscolo—like the story of Winston, above—highlights how geography and the varying cultures of different locales can affect these children's perspective and well-being. After her parents were divorced, Kelly lived for years in conservative Simi Valley, California with her father, who told her that her mother's lesbianism was a "sickness." At age eight, she lost a playmate when the girl's father learned of her mother's sexual orientation. She felt betrayed by and ashamed of her mother, then living in the San Francisco Bay Area with her partner Sue.

But in sixth grade, Kelly started spending summers at her mother's Bay Area home, and found that she felt comfortable there. At a sports camp, she divulged her secret to another girl, who to Kelly's surprise accepted the news with calm indifference. Her next surprise came that evening at dinner when she related the incident and her mother and Sue seemed equally unimpressed. "Are you saying that people here don't care that you're gay?" she asked.

"No, sweetie," her mother replied, "not everyone up here is okay with it." But generally speaking, she said, the Bay Area was significantly more open to diversity than Simi Valley.

Kelly decided to take her last three years of high school living with her mother. But the school was in a mostly white suburb, Lafayette, some miles east (and several notches to the political right) of Berkeley and Oakland. So even there, Kelley knew no one else in school with gay parents, and for a time she continued to be reluctant to tell her friends about her mother. Then she risked it with one girl, who reacted warmly. And since Kelly played basketball, and her mother and Sue attended all her games, "my classmates and their parents were forced to accept that even people in Lafayette could be gay."

She became active with the GSA in her high school, as well as with COLAGE. She blanched when she "heard a homophobic slur in the hallway or saw somebody being picked on because of their supposed sexuality." She now considers herself part of what calls the "incessant struggle" to make society more understanding and accepting:

"Now, however, it is clear to me that the weight I've borne by fighting this never-ending battle has made me a stronger individual. I've learned that standing up for what you believe in may be the most difficult thing you've ever done, but it may also end up being the most rewarding."

6.

Giving Saint Teresa a Run for Her Money

osie O'Donnell has always been out as a lesbian in her private life. But it wasn't until March of 2002, on ABC's *Prime Time* with Diane Sawyer, that she revealed her sexual orientation to a national audience. She told Sawyer that as the mother of three adopted children, she felt compelled to go public when she learned of the troubling plight of Steven Lofton and Roger Croteau.

Because Lofton and Croteau are gay, the State of Florida had undertaken to strip one of their five foster children—all born HIV-positive—from the only family the happy, well-adjusted boy has ever known. If that were to happen to her own son Parker, O'Donnell told Sawyer, "My world would collapse."

The boy, Bert, then ten, is now a healthy teenager described by a school psychologist as "one of the sunniest, most cheerful kids I've ever run across." But as of this writing, in the wake of prolonged litigation, he's still legally in jeopardy of being taken from his thriving family.

The saga that brought television celebrity O'Donnell to the side of Lofton and Croteau—both pediatric nurses and a couple for more than twenty-five years—abounds in poignant ironies.

Social workers, teachers, neighbors, physicians—all who know them—struggle to find superlatives sufficient to describe the quality of the men's parenting. You hear the same adjectives over and again: "Wonderful." "Awesome." "Amazing." "Inspiring." A New York University sociologist, Dr. Judith Stacey, has said of the two men, "They would give Saint Teresa a run for her money."

Both dads are from large families (Steven is one of five children, Roger one of seven), and their own kids' welfare is at the core of their every life decision. The children benefit as well from a small army of aunts, uncles, and cousins—every holiday is an occasion for a large gathering of the extended family—and they spend considerable time at "Camp Grandma," the seventy-five acre farm of Steven's parents.

Despite what turned out to be their obvious dedication and skills, the two men had no intention of becoming parents until urged to do so by a Florida state agency in 1988. Ten years later, the agency, the Children's Home

Society, created an annual honor for outstanding foster parenting, named it the "Lofton-Croteau Award," and gave the first award to its namesakes.

The fathers claim another distinction rare among American parents: They can point to a formal Federal court finding that their family unquestionably possesses the kind of "deeply loving and interdependent relationship" that gives the family unit "its importance to the individuals and to society."

In short, after a state agency first begged the men to become fathers and subsequently knighted them as paragons of parenthood, the same state forced them into a court case that formally found them to be competent and caring parents of the sort that form the backbone of our nation.

But because state law bans homosexual adoption, the court in a bit of strained logic nevertheless went on to uphold the state's right—in "the best interest of Florida's children"!—to take Bert away from the parents, brothers and sister he dearly loves. The irrational decision was affirmed by an appellate court, and in January of 2005, the Supreme Court declined to review the case.

Meanwhile, the Florida bureaucracy has continued to spend large sums, not merely in litigation, but in endless expensive but fruitless investigative attempts to uncover dirt in the two men's background—money that could be spent instead on tackling the state's profound foster care and adoption program shortcomings.

The story of Bert and his two dads ranks as a monument to moral zealotry's potential for ruthless insensitivity.

In early July of 1991, as a nine-week-old infant, Bert lay in a crib in a private room of the upscale Miami Children's Hospital. But the room was off limits to most hospital personnel, and inside the door a line of adhesive tape stretched across the floor as a tacit "do not cross" warning to any staffer unprotected by mask, gown, and latex gloves.

Because his mother was a substance abuser and he was born with HIV antibodies, the child had first been placed in a shelter home, then with foster parents who apparently had a change of heart and dropped him at Children's. There, a frightened staff devoid of experience with AIDS had placed him in virtual isolation while they pleaded with a state placement agency to remove him from their care.

Now a man and a woman stood at the crib, both in street clothes, wearing neither masks nor gloves. The woman was Sema Coppersmith, a social worker with Children's Home Society, an agency of Florida's Department of Children and Families. The man was Steven Lofton who with his life partner Roger Croteau was already a foster parent of three HIV-positive children, all placed with them by Coppersmith. Steven had accompanied Sema to the hospital as a pediatric nurse and interested friend, to help in assessing the child's needs.

The boy's birth certificate said "Caucasian male." But Lofton and Coppersmith laugh as they decide that "he's a pretty tan Caucasian." (In fact, they will learn he is biracial, with an African American father and Puerto Rican mother.)

As Lofton remembers the occasion:

"I was looking at him, looking at his chart, talking with Sema, and we turned around and a nurse said, 'He's ready to go now.' I said, 'We're not taking him, we're just seeing what he needs and she's going to find a home for him.' But the nurse said, 'No, you've got to take him, we're moving him out.'

"Sema had an infant seat in her car, so we decided to take him home and figure out what to do with him."

He pauses, then smiles, "And here we are, fourteen years later."

As he speaks, Steven is sitting at a redwood picnic table in the lush backyard of the family's attractive craftsman prairie-style home in Portland, Oregon, some 3,200 miles from that Miami hospital room. It's 9:30 AM on a morning that started three and a half hours earlier with the two dads supervising what Steven calls a typical "blast off morning" of feeding and grooming five kids and mediating their "fashion fights."

For Steven, rising at 6 AM amounts to sleeping in. Some semesters, he teaches a ten-week water aerobics class at the kids' K-12 school, and then three mornings a week he's up at 5:15. This semester, though, he's teaching the class just one afternoon a week.

Today, at eight o'clock, he had carpooled the kids and some friends to the innovative school that is one of the key reasons he and Roger had picked Portland as their sanctuary after fleeing Florida as what they call "political refugees." There, he parked the family station wagon long enough to take part in a water aerobics class taught by a regular staff member, before returning home to greet the visitors, my wife and me, with whom he now chats.

As the stay-at-home dad, he tends to much of the daily nitty-gritty of parenting. He supervises the kids' age- and ability-assigned chores, attends their swim meets (all five are on swim teams), talks to one or more of their teachers every day, sees to their homework, knows what friends they're biking, swimming, or skateboarding with at any moment, and checks out beforehand any new place they might be going. Roger, despite his job as a pediatric nurse and researcher at Oregon Health and Sciences University, does most of the cooking, and as he told Diane Sawyer of the kids, "They're my life . . .We ended up with a family that no one else wanted and they're wonderful."

Bert is now in his early teens, a natural athlete, gifted dancer, popular student, a boy of infectious enthusiasm. He is also, unlike any of his siblings, free of the HIV virus. In another of the rich ironies in their drama, it was his good health that triggered the events that led the family to seek refuge in Portland.

Bert was found to have "sero-reverted"—he tested free of HIV antibodies—at eighteen months, and as a result the state a few years later formally cleared him for adoption. At the urging of a state case worker, Lofton submitted an application to adopt him. But he had a problem with one question that asked if he was a homosexual.

"When I became a foster parent and filled out forms

an inch thick, the question never appeared. And everyone knew I was gay from the get go." He left the question blank, and the state refused to accept the application because it was incomplete.

So the state started looking for a heterosexual family to take Bert away. By its reasoning, men capable of taking care of the sickest, most unwanted children apparently were not good enough to take care of a boy who was healthy.

Thus began the six-year legal battle that would become something of a national *cause célèbre* and catch the attention of Rosie O'Donnell.

Bert was the fourth of the children to "come home," as Steven and Roger always refer to their kids' arrivals.

The oldest, Frank, came home at eight months with AIDS. He is now a confident seventeen-year-old with a flair for creative writing and painting, a lifeguard both at school and at a neighborhood pool during the summer. He's also the responsible big brother who, in the words of neighbor Gretchen Corbett, "looks after the younger kids with a lot of generosity." (Corbett, once a co-star on TV's *The Rockford Files,* is now the founding director of a Portland nonprofit drama organization for disadvantaged children, and Steven is a member of its board of directors.) Among other things, Frank supervises the complicated medication regime essential to the good health of all but Bert. (Although the other four are still HIV-positive, their virus level is so low as to be technically classified in each case as "virally undetectable.")

Frank was soon followed by two little girls, first Tracy, born a few months before Frank, and then Ginger, a year younger. Despite ongoing academic difficulties, Tracy is affable and outgoing, hard working, popular at school, and talented at various crafts. Ginger—in an era when children born HIV-positive were not expected to live more than two and a half years—was the only one Steven and Roger failed to save; she died in 1994 at age six, her fragile immune system unable to handle a case of measles.

While Frank and Tracy are African American and Bert biracial, the two youngest of the clan, Wayne and Ernie, now eleven and eight, are towheaded biological brothers. They're also the only ones who didn't come home either as infants or in Florida. They were five and two respectively in 1999, when at the recommendation of a Portland pediatrician, Oregon asked Steven and Roger to take the HIV-positive boys suffering also from parental abuse. (To the amusement of their Caucasian fathers, the first reaction of the older children—their dads hadn't thought to alert them—was, "But they're *white*.")

Wayne is an avid reader and especially good at math ("He calculates his allowance months ahead of time," Roger says). Playful, likeable Ernie shows promise of becoming a social lion.

It would be difficult to imagine a family more diverse—what one family friend calls "a census taker's nightmare"—yet more spiritually at-one.

It would be equally difficult, examining the background of the two fathers, to imagine the extraordinary —and inspiring—path their lives have taken.

⁓

Steven and Roger grew up a continent and a cultural world apart, Steven in metropolitan Southern California, Roger in the small southeastern Massachusetts town of Bellingham. Both were raised Catholic and both realized at an early age that they were gay. But the similarities end there.

Both are now in their late forties. Steven is stocky, brown-haired, and speaks in staccato, articulate phrases fueled by a barely contained energy. Roger is leaner, with close-cropped red hair and a reserved, laid-back manner that well serves his dry wit. (Asked by a first-time visitor to their home how they came to acquire so many children, he replies, poker-faced, "You just can't trust the rhythm method.") Steven tends to the flamboyant and arty. His friend Michel Horvat describes the Lofton-Croteau residence, redone by Steven, as a "Portland craftsman turned quasi-Japanese, mid-century-modern-dada-art-gallery of a home." (Horvat is the director of a well-received documentary about the family, titled *We are Dad*.) Roger is task-oriented, measured, and deliberative in approach, befitting the proctor of the family budget and regulator of his mate's inventive impulses. (Steven, he says, suffers from OCRD— Obsessive Compulsive Redecoration Disorder.)

Their sharply contrasting backgrounds and natures have somehow meshed to tame the household's potential for anarchy and shape its wildly diverse characters into a disciplined family full of fun and love.

A close friend, Richard Cardran, remembers Steven as

a youth as "incredibly smart and talented" with "an intensity and independence that always burned hot and fierce." The independence came clear at thirteen, shortly after his parents took him out of school for a planned two month family vacation on a fifty-foot ketch designed and built by his father, the owner of a Long Beach metal fabricating plant. The cruise in fact became a marathon two and a half year globe-circling tour, and Steven, although the youngest, was one of three of the children to jump ship at various ports along the way. He disembarked in Florida, where he stayed for a time with a family friend before returning to California to live with an older sister Dannie, who had also by then like-wise tired of the cruise. He had lost a full academic year, but his brightness soon landed him in a Long Beach magnet school for talented students.

There, Cardran recalls his first sight of Steven: "I saw this thing drive by me in the hallway on roller skates, with glitter all over his face, and wearing some sort of jester outfit with big arms, and tassels hanging every-where." They became instant friends, and Cardran enjoys spinning tales of Steven's antics as a creative jokester. Once, for example, he showed up at a Long Beach pier dressed in drag and wig, carrying a vacuum cleaner that he plugged into a public outlet; after ordering several fisherman aside, he proceeded to vacuum the pier as he sang, "I'm Gonna Wash That Man Right Out Of My Hair." On another occasion, when Steven considered the interior of an older friend's home to be "tacky," he gave away all the furniture to Goodwill one day while the friend was at work—an early example of the redecorating passion that continues to animate Steven to this day.

By comparison, Roger's early years were staid and provincial. He was one of seven redheaded boys (not a single girl!) of Fernand and Juliette Croteau. (His mother, in turn, was one of thirteen survivors of fifteen children delivered by her own mother.) Ironically, his devout Catholic family lived during much of his early life in a home that had once housed an illegal abortion clinic, and he remembers his mother regularly answering the door, tots hanging from every apron string, as a quizzical caller might stammer hesitantly, "But I thought . . .?" All the children attended parochial school, which Roger hated from the beginning, convinced that he was out of sync with its, to him, narrow authoritarian beliefs.

When he was seven, while playing with one of his brothers, Roger suffered second and third degree burns over forty percent of his body when a kerosene can overturned and ignited. Several months in a burn unit and years of reconstructive surgery failed to daunt—perhaps reinforced—his self-reliant spirit. At fourteen, he said farewell to his family's Catholicism and left the parochial school for a public middle school, a job, and essential independence.

Early on, he had decided education would be his ticket out of a little town he considered stifling. After earning a bachelor's degree in business administration and a master's in health care management, he decided to take an associate degree in nursing—both because nursing was then, in the late 1970s, relatively lucrative, and because it offered an easy means of entry into the health care field. And he decided to do it in California, as far away as possible from tiny Bellingham, which even today numbers barely more than twenty thousand souls.

Steven meanwhile had come to the same career decision, via an orthopedic injury that gained him an extended stay in a hospital where he admired a male nurse who became a role model and personal inspiration. It was perhaps a lifesaving decision, giving direction and purpose to a young man described by Cardran as otherwise at serious risk of surrendering to substance abuse. Until then, although "a bundle of creativity who never did anything halfway," Cardran says Steven was "firing in ten directions at once, without focus." In nursing, however, he found his direction in life and cast his energies there with his ingrained passion.

So it was that Steven and Roger met in 1979 at a Victorville, California, nursing school. It was not love at first sight—Roger was seeing someone else. But by the time they finished school, they had become an item and lived together for a time in a home on Lake Arrowhead, where they discovered and adjusted to each other's idiosyncrasies (Steven's compulsive redecorating, for example, and Roger's compulsive punctuality).

But California was in a recession. So they decided to move to Florida, where nurses were in demand, and quickly found jobs as pediatric nurses at Miami's Jackson Memorial Hospital. With two solid salaries and no dependents, they acquired a home in Coral Gables, a small boat, a convertible, and a formidable collection of high-living, mostly single, mixed gay-and-straight, friends.

In the mid-'80s, fate intruded, in the form of the rampaging AIDS epidemic that brought the hospital an increasing number of AIDS babies whose mothers were dying or incapable of caring for them. They were thought of generally as throwaways, as medical waste, either isolated in cramped hospital cribs or placed in temporary foster homes for their predictably short lives of a few months to, at best, a few years. But Roger in particular found he liked the colleagues he worked with in the pediatric AIDS ward, and at the same time was appalled by the fear—more accurately, panic—demonstrated by other hospital workers around the children. Working with AIDS babies became the two men's mission.

At this point, in 1985, Steven's good friend Richard Cardran became an unwitting actor in the unfolding of the drama that would capture national attention. Cardran had moved to New York but had become ill, unable to work, and saw his insurance coverage cut off when tests disclosed he had full-blown AIDS, which had claimed the life of his domestic partner three years earlier. Assuming he had only months to live, he moved back to California and lived for a time with a woman friend in Los Angeles. Then he got a telephone call from Steven and Roger, who bluntly demanded, "Get your ass out here. We'll take care of you."

Knowing the two men, Cardran wasn't surprised. "They're into rescues," he says. "I'm alive because of them. I wouldn't have made it otherwise." And he calls himself, "Adoptee Zero," the first to be rescued by them from AIDS in a kind of home training course for the ill infants to come.

Roger and Steven assumed at the time that Cardran was "circling the drain"—part of the black-humor terminology they had adopted as a self-protective mechanism in the face of so much tragedy. But the two were by then known and respected throughout the AIDS treatment network, both for their frequent open criticism of doctors who, out of fear, hesitated to treat AIDS patients, and for their awareness of the latest developments.

"They fed me, they clothed me," Richard says, "and they never asked a thing in return." Ultimately, they would also help him get the first AIDS drug, AZT, through a Federal program. Slowly, he came to a new awareness and, "At some point, I realized I wasn't dying and it was time to restart my engine." Today, he is an award winning media designer and technologist and co-founder of a software applications firm. (In 2002, Cardran was named one of the fifty most influential people in the interactive broadcasting field known as "streaming"; in 2004 he won an Emmy for Outstanding Achievement in Interactive Television.)

Before he left Miami, however, Richard had bonded with the latest member of the Lofton-Croteau household— the little boy who to this day he calls "Frankie," and who came home in 1987, the first of the Lofton-Croteau kids, while Richard was living there. Richard is lavish in his praise of Frank ("I always liked him from the get-go.") as a boy with "great personality" who is "easy-going, sensitive and highly creative" in both art and writing. And Richard takes pride in the thought that caring for Richard helped prepare Steven and Roger to tend to Frank and Tracy, who were soon to follow.

The immediate agent of Frank's coming home was Sema Coppersmith of the Children's Home Society, who had become a one-woman crusader in search of good homes for as many of the AIDS babies as possible. When she asked Steven and Roger to become foster parents, their first reaction, despite their dismay at the children's pitiful state, had been negative. They had always loved kids—other people's kids—but had never given a thought to parenting for themselves. But as Frank's mother lay near death in the hospital, she herself begged Steven to care for her child, and her dying wish carried the day.

Still, their decision was not to become parents—only temporary caretakers. Since AIDS babies were presumed doomed, caring for such a child for some months sounded more like around-the-clock nursing—loving and making him comfortable until he died—than fathering. A future that included driver's training or advice on dating (truly critical when your child is HIV-positive) was then hardly part of the plan.

So Steven became a licensed foster parent; and at the insistence of the state, because caring for a child with AIDS is so demanding, quit his job—temporarily, he assumed.

Within months, Frank was joined by Tracy, who had had twelve hospitalizations before coming home. Among other things, she had a sinus problem so severe that the men had to suction her as many as four times a night to keep her breathing.

Then one day Sema handed Roger another little girl, Ginger, and Roger decided he wanted her. In Michel Horvat's words, "Roger figured the best way to sell Steven on Ginger was packaging." He wrapped her in swaddling clothes, placed her in a large rattan basket, put the basket on their front porch, rang the bell and ran. Steven answered the ring— "And there was this baby on the doorstep." She turned out to be a happy, fun-loving child who loved to read and, after Bert came home when she was four, to push her little brother in his stroller. Bert was only two when she died, but she's still mourned by the men and the two older children.

By this time, they were committed parents who loved their kids deeply. But the role at first fit somewhat uneasily. And Cardran speculates that the initial motivation, at least for Steven, the full-time parent, was probably a mixed one. "He genuinely loved Frank and Tracy. You have to. But it was also a kind of in-your-face thing: 'I'm gay and I have two black kids—get over it.' But there's been a transformation to one hundred percent dedication."

Steven would appear to agree. "At first," he says, "having kids was sort of a novelty. But still, it felt nat-ural, and my parental feelings and my confidence grew. I had cared for kids in the hospital of all ages and abili-ties. So taking an infant home wasn't peculiar. But it *was* different. This was twenty-four hours a day."

The men's lifestyle changed drastically in other ways too. Now they seldom saw their earlier closest group of friends, composed mainly of singles and childless cou-ples: "They liked to do things on the spur of the moment and we couldn't do that."

For the children, it meant going from solitary confinement in an institutional crib to what Steven describes as "an abundance of contact": When the children were little, they "would never touch the ground"—just go from arm to arm.

At first, there were no medications for the children, and it would be years before any at all would be available in Miami. But in 1991, the men took the initiative to enroll the kids in a National Institutes of Health study of AZT, the first antiviral AIDS medication. Between 1991 and 1995, the men and children made some thirty trips to Washington, D.C. for stays of a day to a week at the Bethesda, Maryland NIH campus.

To this day, the routine of dispensing and downing dozens of pills is a critical part of the daily family routine for all the children but Bert. The other four have their medication schedules down pat. One day in Florida, this caused a brief flare-up after a mother saw Frank taking his pills on a school field trip. She asked him why, he told her he had AIDS, and on their return she complained to the principal. But her grievance received short shrift. "He's welcome at this school," she was told.

In part, that reaction was due to a Dade County provision banning antigay discrimination. But in large part, also, it was due to the dads' proactive stance. They had made certain from the outset that the school administrators and the kids' teachers were fully aware of their situation. Roger was president and Steven vice president of the Parent-Teacher Student Association.

For a typical family, the challenges of seeing to five

children, twenty-four hours seven days a week, is no easy task. But the added complications for Steven and Roger would seem monumental. If the children don't take their medications on time, they build up resistance and the drugs might not work. Some have to be taken with food, so when it's meal time, it's mealtime—exclamation point, period. Coordinating all of this with getting five children to school, to swim class, to doctor's appointments, and so on, means that in some respects the house has to be run like a military camp. As a result of their early abuse at the hands of their birth parents, the two younger children require special attention, including weekly psychotherapy sessions followed by consultations with the therapist by the two dads.

And of course, Steven's elegance of taste precludes in any event the sight of a child clothed in mismatched colors schemes (one source of the daily "fashion fights"), and no house of his could be anything but artfully maintained and lushly landscaped. And it's all done under the scrutiny of two states' child protection services —with one of the states, Florida, itching to find something amiss.

But it's also done with humor, grace, and love, tacitly attested to by the tenderness of the goodnight tucks-and-kisses, the happy hugs and greetings on return from school.

Soon after the first kids came home, Roger also left his job at Jackson Memorial and founded a special-needs day care center, modeled along Head Start program lines, that is still operated today by the Children's Home Society. It's housed in a building designed pro bono, at

Roger's urging, by a nationally known architectural firm—"a beautiful building, serving the most unwanted kids in Miami," in Steven's phrase.

In Portland, both men now teach part-time (Steven water aerobics, Roger cooking) at their children's school. Steven has served on its board and is active in its PTA. And—another touch of irony—both remain on the board of a Florida Head Start preschool the children once attended.

In part, their close ties to the kids' schools serve as a defensive measure, putting them in strategic position to detect early warning signs of trouble. But they have chosen the schools carefully, and have encountered virtually no problems there. For most of the years in Florida, the children were so young that their peers weren't really aware of their unusual situation. Roger laughs as he recalls one Halloween when Tracy's costume included a tiara of Steven's: "The kids were all admiring it and Tracy, then six, said, 'Oh, it's my dad's.' And the only thing they said was, 'And he lets you wear it?' None of the kids thought twice about why Steven had a tiara."

Now, in Portland they have found a school where diversity is not only accepted but is the order of the day.

Most neighbors are likewise fully accepting, but on a few occasions have displayed an unfortunate ignorance about sexual orientation and AIDS. One seemingly intelligent but perplexed older woman asked Steven, "How did you give the children AIDS?" His careful attempt at education fell short: "She wouldn't have anything to do with us."

Another time Bert, then eight, came home from a bike ride in a park, upset and scratched up. He was reluctant to say what had happened, but finally admitted he had gotten into a scrape with another boy who said, "Your dad's gay." Bert shoved him, saying, "No, he's not." Steven recalls:

"I told him, 'Well, I'm sorry he said that, but I *am* gay and that's what people do sometimes.' And Bert looked at me and said, 'You *are* gay?' I said, 'You don't know what that means, do you, honey?' We had never talked about it. But he thought it was bad, though he had no idea what it meant." So Bert got his explanation—"gay" simply referred to a man who loves another man, or a woman who loves another woman.

Sema Coppersmith, the social worker who placed four children with Steven and Roger, describes them as "a very unique, loving, caring family." It was her agency, the Children's Home Society, that created the Lofton-Croteau Award for outstanding foster parenting because, she says, the two men were "incredible not only with regard to their own kids but with helping other foster parents also." She says their children "have been exposed to everything you could possibly want your own children to be exposed to." She still keeps in touch with the men, and calls them "wonderful, wonderful, wonderful people."

In Florida, the serious problems began after Steven's adoption application was rejected. When Bert was five and in kindergarten, a sympathetic teacher called to alert the fathers that someone from the state was taking pictures of the boy. Steven contacted a state official who told him their pictures showed that Bert "was not being cared for, he wasn't wearing socks." It was probably true that Bert wasn't wearing socks—he didn't like wearing socks and would take them off. But this was hot and humid Miami, where half the class wore no socks and many wore thongs. But the lack of socks apparently was the only thing officials could find to complain about.

Shortly thereafter, Steven says, the state sent a very aggressive case worker who "wanted Bert out of the house." After that, he got sporadic calls saying that the caseworker was looking for a home for him: "The heat was on."

The "heat" stems from a Florida law initiated by an earlier celebrity, a pop singer and Miss America runner-up named Anita Bryant, perhaps best known for her 1970s television commercials promoting orange juice. In 1977, Bryant parlayed her fame into a successful "Save Our Children" campaign to repeal a Miami ordinance banning antigay discrimination, and followed that with another crusade that led the state legislature to pass a law banning gays from adopting children. Her argument: "Since gays can't produce, they must recruit and freshen their ranks." (Roger looks at his three avowedly heterosexual teenagers and shrugs, "I don't know where we went wrong.")

Social worker Coppersmith decries the law: "What makes them less of a parent than anyone else? You should be with a husband and wife where maybe the husband beats up on the wife and children—I guess that's the philosophy." Of those who actually knew the men in Florida, she says, "Everyone was charmed by Steven and Roger and loved them. But we were dealing with the State of Florida."

Under Federal law, foster parents are free to move from state to state, so long as the children remain subject to the laws of the state that placed the children. So when the dads decided to move to Portland—because of its relatively accepting social climate, the especially progressive K-12 school available to all of the children, and its proximity to Steven's parents off the Oregon coast—Bert remained at the mercy of the state of Florida and the courts.

They quickly settled into the red brick, green-roofed home in an attractive neighborhood on a bluff over-looking the Willamette River and downtown Portland, and with the kids set about planting its now neatly man-icured landscaping featuring a dizzying panoply of flowers, evergreens, and plants.

Within a few months, they were asked by their new state to take Wayne and Ernie from Eugene, Oregon. The two brothers had been severely abused by their drug-addicted parents and the so-called Vampire Cult to which the parents belonged, and were in urgent need of health care. The abuse had left them in horrific condi-tion, behaving so wildly that the state had resorted to drugging them, and they arrived refusing to ingest any-thing but soda. Originally, Steven says, the placement was thought to be temporary. "The idea was to get them here to Portland, get them healthy, and then the state would find a home for them." That was seven years ago.

In Portland, the men found a cultural climate at stark odds with Florida. They describe Portland as "very progressive" and "very pro-child" and the case workers as "terrific."

In Portland, for example, a caseworker told them that Florida had asked for some pictures of Bert. "That's weird," said the caseworker, "I'm not going to do it."

Free from direct harassment by the Florida case workers, if not from the reach of the state's legal claim—Steven at one point, for example, had to travel to Florida and undergo a grueling marathon deposition seemingly aimed at uncovering character flaws—they settled into the routines of what Steven calls a "real traditional household."

⁓

"They know their full expectations," Steven says of the kids' active home life. House chores and bedtimes go by age and ability. At meal time, for example, since Wayne and Ernie aren't tall enough to reach the dishes, Wayne sorts the silverware and Ernie puts napkins on the table, while the older kids split the table-setting and cleanup duties. Likewise, Wayne and Ernie sort the laundry after the older ones manage the washing and drying.

As Bert told Diane Sawyer, "We all work as a team. We're all a unit."

The kids say they appreciate Roger's cooking and handyman talents, and on *Prime Time* Tracy even complimented Steven's ability "to pick out the right clothes that matches." Steven found that to be a particularly

welcome compliment in light of the almost daily refer-
eeing of squabbles over what they should wear.

The men decided early on that television "should be a
controlled substance," although they do play tapes on
the VCR and go out to movies frequently.

"Seriously, we really don't have time for TV," Steven
says. The family is physically active every day. "If we
don't go to the pool, we ride bikes or skateboard." In the
evening, when homework is done, they play games and
do puzzles. On weekends or holidays, they might take in
an amusement park or travel to a nearby beach.

Still, he confesses, you can't get away from TV: "It's
everywhere. At a neighbor's house. When we go to the hospital for an appointment, or to the barber shop, the TV is
on. Everywhere you go." But he doesn't think the kids feel
deprived. "We have so much going on, and they have
access to it elsewhere."

They often have friends for dinner, and the holidays are
always spent with extended family. Three consecutive
Easters have been highlighted by egg hunts at the home of
Steven's sister and brother-in-law in nearby Eugene.
Thanksgiving is usually at home, with a large gathering
that includes Steven's parents and various of his brothers
and sisters and their families. The extended family also
gathers for an outdoor barbecue on either Memorial Day
or Labor Day. Halloween is "a big deal" with costumes and
trick-or-treating: "Tracy wants to go to parties, everyone
else wants to trick-or-treat." Christmas, as Steven puts it,
"We swap all over." Sometimes it's at the elder Loftons'
farm outside Corvallis, Oregon. One year, though—the
only time in ten years Steven's parents weren't able to join

them for the holidays—they spent Christmas with an uncle of Steven's in California.

One recent summer, Tracy spent some weeks at "Camp Grandma," helping the grandparents paint the walls of some rooms, doing yardwork and shopping in nearby Newport. The following summer, Bert spent every other weekend working on the farm, while Frank and Tracy, for the second straight year, went on a five-day river raft trip. (Roger convinced a corporation to sponsor the annual trip for HIV teenagers; joined by a psychiatrist, psychologist, and counselor, the youngsters discuss sexuality and relationships, and talk freely and in depth about how HIV affects their lives.) The rest of that summer, Frank worked as a lifeguard at nearby Columbia neighborhood pool. The younger kids were all active with their respective summer swim teams.

Since Roger's parents are older and now have difficulty traveling, each year the men take the kids to visit his folks, Fernand and Juliette, in Massachusetts. The elder Croteaus also joined Roger, Steve and the three younger children (Frank and Tracy were on their river raft trip) on a week-long R Family Cruise (see chapter 2) in the summer of 2004. Roger generally flies by himself two or three additional times a year to see them. Occasionally, as during one recent spring vacation, Roger takes the five kids without Steven.

How does a lone parent handle five youngsters on a long cross-country plane trip? "It used to be almost impossible," Roger says, "but now it's easy"—thanks to Nintendo Game-boys: "They sit for hours without moving. It's just incredible." And the kids get a special treat at the East Coast grandparents' home—they get to watch television. They also get to camp out in sleeping bags and bike and skateboard with some neighbor boys who happen to be about the same age as Roger's three older ones. One year they toured Cape Cod with their dads and Fernand and Juliette, including a visit to Provincetown, where the nine of them joined hundreds of other families with same-sex parents at the annual gathering of the international Family Pride Coalition and its offshoot youth organization COLAGE (Children of Lesbians and Gays Everywhere). (See chapters 2 and 5.)

As of the last check, dating had not yet complicated the family life, though Steven and Roger say Frank is clearly attracted to girls and Tracy to boys. But so far their teenage socializing has been primarily with groups of nonpaired boys and girls. Roger says Bert, Wayne, and Ernie "are too young" for sexual interests—"They like Legos"—although Bert identifies as heterosexual.

⁓

If the family is traditional in its daily routines, it is of course wildly untraditional both in its makeup and special challenges. The kids are all foster-parented, and only the younger two are biologically related. Two are black, a third biracial and dark-skinned, with white parents. The parents are gay. All but Bert have AIDS. Their family is embroiled in controversial high-profile litigation. (The Federal appeals court opinion in their case correctly noted that as of January 2004, the family's "story has been chronicled in dozens of news stories and editorials as well as on national television.")

In short, in almost any typical middle-class school in the nation, they would simultaneously trigger virtually every possible peer prejudice.

So for Steven and Roger, finding the right schools for the children has always commanded high priority. And in Portland, their prospecting turned up a public school almost as nontraditional as their family. Moreover, because it is K–12, all the kids can attend the same school. And because parents are encouraged to become involved, both men are actively engaged there. As mentioned above, Steven is a volunteer and conducts a regular ten-week water aerobics class, while Roger teaches occasional cooking classes by taking a half day off work. (According to Steven, Roger's classes are a "raging success—the kids line up to get in.")

The school is known as the Metropolitan Learning Center, located in an unlovely 1914 brick building in largely commercial Northwest Portland, its condition perhaps somewhat understated in city school district reports as "Needs Upgrade." But despite its unprepossessing appearance, the school maintains a long waiting list and consistently pulls down the district's highest "exceptional" school rating in student performance categories. Parents are willing to drive as much as twenty-five miles, much of it through downtown rush hour traffic, to deliver their children there each morning.

Inside, a visitor might spot a twelve-year-old, alone, reading a book while pacing up and down a hallway. In a classroom, a multi-aged group listens to a parent describe his or her work as a surgeon, or an auto mechanic, or a salesperson, or a filmmaker. In a hallway corner, a ten-year-old stands hand-in-hand with a teacher who might be explaining a fine point of mathematics—or perhaps how the student's remarks hurt another child's feelings.

If you were there in March of 2004, when the county issued marriage licenses to some three thousand same-sex couples, you could hardly have missed a large banner hanging from the transom of one openly gay staffer's office, the words "Just Married" hand-painted in bright red.

A school publication emphasizes "flexible approaches to learning," and each student's "personal choice" as a "key educational ingredient." A counselor underscores the approach that some might be tempted to describe more as "radical" than merely "flexible." "We don't have grades," she says. Instead, teachers draft reports summarizing accomplishments and "concerns" for each student. Children as young as six choose elective afternoon classes. By the time they're nine, they're probably taking electives (which might range from bowling to fine arts to Roger's cooking class) with a mix of older children. Everybody—children, teachers and parents alike—goes by first name. Gifted students tutor those with learning disabilities.

All the Lofton-Croteau kids appear to be thriving at the school, where diversity is the standard. Racial, ethnic, or cultural slurs are a strict no-no. Several of their classmates have gay or lesbian parents, some teachers are openly gay or lesbian, and the student body reflects a broad ethnic and economic mix. Homosexual staffers and parents, with their children, get together regularly for pot luck suppers.

To a traditionalist, all this might smack of educational anarchy. But the school ranks high by any standard measure such as the SAT scores of those who go on to college. And whether the goal be rocket science or household plumbing, the school's aim is to prepare each student for a career that will be personally gratifying.

Frank, for example, expects to go on to college, while for Tracy, a traditional school might have ruled out the possibility of any career whatever. But here, she's discovered a flair for crafts. And after a school field trip to a Women in Trades Career Fair, where she saw women who run businesses as plumbers, electricians, carpenters, and other trades, she started thinking about a similar career. So back at school, she enrolled in a class taught by a contractor, where every afternoon the children loaded a van with tools and went to work on houses being rehabilitated under a city program.

"Some of the other girls in the class are a little hesitant to get under the sink and start unscrewing the pipe," Steven says. "But she dives right in and loves it." Gretchen Corbett, who lives across the street from the Lofton-Croteau family and knows all the children well, seconds Steven's observation: "Tracy's a really good worker. I wouldn't be a bit surprised if she's able to build houses."

After Steven and Roger became one of the county's first same-sex couples to obtain marriage licenses and were married by a minister at a wedding attended by the kids in a downtown public auditorium, Bert excitedly told all his classmates about it the next day.

It was something of a contrast from his reaction at the supper table a few days before the wedding, when the men first mentioned their plans. Bert looked up surprised and said, "You guys aren't married yet?" Apparently, he had always just assumed that *all* parents, by definition, are married.

⁓

The family seldom talk about the State of Florida's threat, and his dads assure Bert, "Nobody's going to come get you." Steven and Roger say the effect of the high-profile litigation has been minimal. "They feel secure here," Steven says. "They have parents. They have two sets of grandparents. They've always had a house. They've never felt insecure for lack of anything."

Meanwhile, however, Florida retains its legal claim to Bert, underscoring the potentially devastating effects of misguided moralism. And while Steven and Roger are reluctant to discuss the matter, Richard Cardran says that throughout the litigation, the state relentlessly dug for dirt, and the men "got a lot of death threats" and telephone calls deriding them as "pedophiles, fags, perverts." Cardran think they remain unmoved because they see the cause as "one more thing that needs saving."

If the state's indifference to Bert's best interest seems irrational, it might be explained simply as a holdover from an earlier era's relative ignorance and the influence of a popular and beautiful television personality. But the contemporary approval of that irrationality by two Federal courts reveals the extent to which the cultural bias at the core of Anita Bryant's crusade continues to sway our society and its institutions.

As the lead plaintiff with three other gay men whose adoption applications had similarly been refused, Steven filed suit against the state in 1999, when Bert was eight, asking that its ban against gay adoption be declared unconstitutional.

In a pretrial deposition, Steven summarized his relationship to Bert (who was identified in the court proceedings as "John Doe") as follows:

John is my son. I am committed to caring for him and providing for all his needs. I have been his parent in every way. For example, every day, I wake him up in the morning and help him get dressed and ready to go to school; I help him with his homework when he comes home from school; we have a family dinner together every night, cooked by Roger; and we spend our evenings engaged in a variety of family activities. I take care of John when he is sick. I make sure all his vaccinations are up to date. I am a parent volunteer in John's class once a week and an active P.T.S.A. member. I try to expand his horizons by taking him on trips. I encourage him to pursue the positive, healthy activities that he enjoys, such as swim team and drama. I provide a child-friendly home. I include John's friends in our family, inviting them over for dinner and having them join us on family outings to the beach or park. Roger and I teach John household responsibilities such as yard work, car maintenance and cooking. I discipline him appropriately when he misbehaves. I hug and comfort him when he is upset. I teach him manners, respect and other values that I consider important. I make sure he is safe. He calls me "Dad."

Steven's lawyers asked to put on actual trial evidence of the nature of Bert's relationship to Steven, Roger, and the other kids. The Court seemed to be getting off to a good start when it held that that was unnecessary, because it was perfectly obvious that the relationship was of the deeply loving type that in general makes the family unit so integral to society.

In a cogent paragraph that would necessarily seem to open the door to a decision in Steven's favor, the Court made a number of excellent points: What makes a family is not "mere biological ties," but the "emotional attachments that derive from the intimacy of daily association." Those attachments determine a family's importance both "to the individual members involved and to society." This is particularly true, moreover, with respect to children like Bert, who have never "known their biological parents." Hence, the Court had no doubt that the tie between Bert and Steven was "as close as those between biological parents" nor that theirs was a "deeply loving and interdependent relationship" involving "intimate, highly personal parent-child" relations.

In the very next sentence, however, the Court slammed the door shut. All this love, intimacy, and interdependence, it turns out, is beside the point. Rather, the Court held, "the existence of strong emotional bonds between [Steven and Bert] does not inherently grant them a fundamental right to family privacy, intimate association and family integrity." Since the state had given Bert to Steven, it retained the right to take him away. Unlike biological parents, foster parents "do not have a justifiable expectation of an enduring companionship *because the emotional ties originate under state law.*" (The italics are mine and not in the Court's decision.)

Get it? Those emotional ties weren't really forged by human beings, like Steven, Bert, and the others. They were at root, rather, created by some words on a page of the Florida legal code. Thus, with a sweep of the judicial pen, the years of mutual love and of constant attention, feeding, clothing, tucking-in, hugging, laughing, scolding, et cetera, et cetera, all became legally irrelevant. With such personal matters out of the way, the Court found it relatively easy as a technical matter to decide that it was not unreasonable—and therefore was constitutional—for the state to decide that other things equal, married heterosexual couples make the best parents.

Never mind that only in a perfect world would other things ever be equal. Never mind, for example, that about one-quarter (23 percent) of Florida's adoptions were in fact made *not* to married couples but to single parents; after all, the Court reasoned, since those single parents presumably were heterosexual, there was always the chance they *might* someday *get* married.

And, most crucially, never mind that a law admitted by the Court to have been designed in "the best interests of the child" was here being wielded by the state in an attempt to savage the life of a little boy who, by the Court's own finding, was already in a "deeply loving and interdependent relationship" with the only parents and only family he had ever known.

Steven and fellow plaintiffs appealed the decision to a three-judge Federal court in Atlanta. By the time the case was briefed, argued, and finally decided in January of 2004, Bert was just three months shy of his thirteenth birthday. In its forty-seven page opinion, the appellate court devoted a single sentence to the lower court's findings as to the "deeply loving and interdependent" nature of the relationship between Steven and Bert: "By all accounts," the Court wrote, " Lofton's efforts in caring for [his foster] children have been exemplary." That fact, however, was plainly irrelevant to the Court and never again mentioned in its exhaustive analysis of various technical nuances of constitutional law. Like that of the lower court, its holding was based on the notion that the state legislature could reasonably conclude that it is in the best interest of adoptive children "to be placed in a home anchored by both a father and a mother."

The true motivation behind the decision, however, shows up in the last two sentences of the opinion, where the Court in effect admits that it simply considers homosexual adoption too hot a political potato for the judiciary to get involved:

"Thus, any argument that the Florida legislature was misguided in its decision is one of legislative policy, not constitutional law. The legislature is the proper forum for this debate, and we do not sit as a superlegislature 'to award by judicial decree what was not achievable by political consensus.'"

In other words, so long as a substantial proportion of voters have no problem with treating gays and lesbians as something less than equally entitled citizens, incidental cruelty to little children and their families is, as a matter of law, simply beside the point.

As a practical matter, Steven and Roger shrug off the adverse court decisions. They assume that potential real life adoptive parents are more sensible than the courts. As Roger asks:

"Why would anyone want to take a teenage child away from a good home? You're asking for a problem. The fact is, it's psychologically unsound to pull a young boy from a happy home. And of course, anyone who'd want to do that, there's something really wrong with them."

Is there also maybe "something really wrong" with a state government that wants to do that very thing?

On the *Prime Time* show featuring the Lofton-Croteau family, Diane Sawyer asked Florida Representative Randy Ball, who supports the gay adoption ban, "What makes great parents?"

The important things, Ball said, are that the parents "love each other" and that they give top priority to "the interest of the child."

It was another sad irony in the Lofton-Croteau case. According to Sawyer, state officials and childcare officials all turned down ABC's request to voice their views, and Ball was the only one of twenty-four state legislators who would agree to do so. So the lone voice to speak up on Florida's behalf, while expressly defending the state's refusal to allow Steven and Roger to be adoptive parents, defined "good parent" in terms that might have been invented to describe the same two men.

Giving Saint Teresa a Run for Her Money.

The Lofton-Croteau clan poses with Diane Sawyer after their appearance on ABC's *Primetime Live* in 2002. Back row, from left: Bert, Tracy, Diane Sawyer, Frank, Steven Lofton, and Roger Croteau. Front: Wayne, left, and Ernie. (Chapter 6)

Diaper Sales Are Up in "P-Town."

Long a legendary summer playground for single gay and lesbian couples, Provincetown, Massachusetts, now additionally hosts hundreds of same-sex family members at the annual Family Week of the Family Pride Coalition. Above, Marie Longo, left, and Allison Bauer, with their twins, Joshua and Rebecca Bauer Longo, at a recent Family Week parade down Commercial Street. (Chapter 2)

Margaret O'Brien

Sarah Gray

"There's So Much Love in Our Family."

Top: Alex Tinker, left, and Josh Graham stand behind Connie Tinker, Maya Graham, Bonnie Tinker, Sara Graham, and Cierra Graham. (The pets are Star, on leash, and Angel.) Bottom: Bonnie and Sara at their 2004 wedding "under the care," in Quaker terminology, of Multnomah Friends Meeting. (Chapter 1)

The Grooms and Maid of Honor.

Sal Iacullo, left, and Wayne Steinman were legally married in
Toronto, Canada, in 2003 with daughter Hope at their side. Three
years earlier, they held a more formal wedding ceremony in Vermont, with the then twelve-year-old Hope as maid of honor.
(Chapter 3)

Robert Mehaffie

"Classroom Party Parent."

That's how dad Tim Fisher was known to his children's elementary school classmates and their parents. Celebrating Christmas above are "Poppa" Scott Davenport (top), Tim and daughter Kati (middle), and son Fritz. Tim's "Daddy" stocking is hidden behind Scott. (Chapter 3)

"Something Right Happened in That Family."

Portland, Oregon, Mayor Tom Potter poses unofficially with two
of his city's police officers, Katie Potter, left, and Pam Moen, and
two of his nine grandchildren, Madison and McKenzie Potter-
Moen. (Chapter 4)

"Four amazing, loving parents."

That's how Avi, center, and Danielle Naparsteck Silber, right, describe their two lesbian mothers and two gay dads. Here, they celebrate a recent New Year's with biological mother Susan Silber, the city attorney of Takoma Park, Maryland. (Chapter 7)

The "Gastro-Evangelist" and His Family.

Andrew Warner, right, is a United Church of Christ minister in Milwaukee, Wisconsin, where his congregation benefits among other things from his dedication and expertise as a chef. Above, "Daddy" Andrew and "Papa" Jay Edmundson hold their adopted Guatemalan-born sons, David, left, and Tomas. (Chapter 8)

7.

The Triumph of Devotion

Certain circumstances are generally believed, often with good reason, to be detrimental to children's emotional health:

If their parents become separated.
If their parents are of different religions.
If their parents are of different races.
Or, many would argue, if they're raised in a home headed by two parents of the same sex.

Well, meet Danielle and Avi Naparsteck Silber. They've

grown up subject to every one of those "ifs." By conventional standards, moreover, their family's structure is so wildly off the mainstream mark that it once launched a domestic court judge on a fruitless search for applicable legal precedent.

Danielle and Avi, however, are doing just fine, thank you. And once you've mapped the labyrinthian contours of their family arrangement, you're at the starting point of an unusual tale of parental devotion.

Danielle and Avi each say, with obviously deeply felt conviction, that they have "four amazing, loving parents," namely, two lesbian mothers and two gay fathers. Technically, they misspeak. In the eyes of the law, they have just two parents: their biological mother and, under their state's "second-parent adoption law," her domestic partner of twenty-two years.

Their two mothers, however, are now separated. Their biological mother and biological father are of different religions. The children are white but say the father most intimately involved with the details of their day-to-day lives is black. And he and their biological father, like their two mothers, are also now separated.

In this seeming sea of domestic, ethnic, and religious turbulence, two islands of interpersonal stability have nevertheless provided the foundation for healthy childhood growth. First, whatever their personal differences, the four parents' respect for one another remains undiminished. And, above all, all four remain unswerving in their deep, ongoing commitment to the children's welfare.

The result is two apparently well-rounded, solidly

grounded, high-performing, outgoing, friendly young people.

In high school, Danielle was class president her last two years, a television producer for the school network, a singer and actor in school productions, and a three-year member of the soccer team. As I write, she is a senior honor student at Washington University in St. Louis, where among a variety of other activities, she was instrumental in the founding of both an international human rights film festival and a social justice organization creating partnerships between college students and area high school students. As a junior, she spent a term in Kenya and now speaks fluent Kiswahili, which she put to use living with Swahili families with whom—while furthering her study of their cultural, political, and spiritual histories—she herded goats, milked cows, carried water from springs and wells, and cleaned goat and cow pens. She plans to apply for a Fulbright Foreign Scholarship to further her international research. She is a national director of COLAGE (Children of Lesbians and Gays Everywhere). A high-profile career in one or more areas of human rights would surprise none who know her.

Avi at sixteen, despite some earlier learning problems, has become an honor student, and is a talented chess player. He's also deep into electronics and computers, a member of a variety of organizations, and an alumnus of a fourteen-and-under community soccer league. He has a keen sense of humor and an easy self-confidence rare in boys his age.

At center stage of the unlikely drama are the children's biological mother Susan Silber, a lawyer and longtime city attorney of Takoma Park, Maryland, and their adoptive mother Dana Naparsteck, a county social worker. Their biological father is Chris Hennin, a Washington, D.C., educator and businessman who speaks five languages, has taken the lead in exposing the children to cultural events and frequent vacation travel (often to such distant destinations as Paris and Australia), and has inspired their interest in international matters. Still, the man Danielle has described as "more the day-to-day father" is Art Thomas, a Web manager at the World Bank and Chris's former domestic partner.

The children grew up in Takoma Park, and their mothers might well echo the classic real estate adage by labeling three of the key ingredients in successful same-sex parenting as "location, location, and location." Takoma Park, which abuts the District of Columbia, is now an unselfconsciously gay-friendly village just a few miles across the Potomac River from the state of Virginia, where same-sex partnering is still officially treated as unlawful.

But Takoma Park's evolution into what its residents affectionately refer to as the People's Republic of Takoma Park—and most specifically the town's easy acceptance of families headed by gays and lesbians—owes much to the efforts of Susan and Dana themselves. As a proactive openly lesbian city official, Susan bolstered and advanced Takoma Park's progressive potential. As a team, the mothers' careful planning and confident modeling of their family values smoothed the social path not only for themselves but for the other families like theirs who would subsequently find Takoma Park a welcoming place.

But not even Takoma Park could shield Danielle and Avi from all of the pitfalls created by conventional attitudes toward their "different" family.

—◦

Susan grew up in New Jersey, earned a BA at the University of Michigan and a law degree from State University of New York at Buffalo. There she met Dana, then an undergraduate, and they began what would become a twenty-two year domestic partnership. Shortly after becoming a couple, they moved to Washington, D.C., so that Dana could complete a master's in social work at nearby University of Maryland. In Washington, Susan was a clinical fellow at the District's Antioch Law School, where among other things, she ran a women's rights clinic that helped found a national coalition to fight wage discrimination.

They always knew they wanted children, and moved to Takoma Park because of its more suburban setting and because of the top-rated Montgomery County school system. There, Susan joined an older male lawyer in a two-person practice, and when her law partner became city attorney in 1981 she thereby became the de facto assistant city attorney. After her partner resigned a few years later, she gained the Council's nod over eighty-one other candidates to replace him as city attorney.

From the beginning, both were wholly out as lesbians. For some years, until the birth of Danielle, Dana was also on a career track as a community organizer, serving among other things as a YWCA program director. The

pair quickly became an accepted part of the city's professional and social circles. One of their favorite pictures
shows them with a huge bouquet of flowers sent to the
hospital at Danielle's birth by the City Council, together
with the Council's formal certificate of congratulations.

As city attorney, Susan helped spark a series of progressive measures of the kind that brought the town that
"People's Republic" tag. In 1986, for example, the city
approved a collective bargaining bill giving city
employees an unusually broad right to strike. The
Council also ensured that the definition of "immediate
family" in the city code included domestic partners for
all purposes, including equal treatment with spouses
regarding city personnel benefits.

And in 1991, Susan and a councilman launched a
series of forums on gay families that culminated two
years later when Takoma Park became the state's first
municipality to extend health insurance benefits to
domestic partners of city employees.

The town by then was becoming well-known as a
comfortable enclave for lesbians and gay men, who now
comprise a significantly higher proportion of the population than any other community in Montgomery
County. It's a demographic reality unquestionably
inspired in important part by the image of a wholly out
lesbian city attorney making clear that Takoma Park
welcomed diversity.

From the outset, they knew that they wanted their
children to know their father *as* a father. Their search
for someone who would act as more than mere donor led
them through friends to Chris Hennin. After several

months of discussion, they agreed to a set of informal guidelines that ultimately would apply to both their children. The women accepted the full financial burden and gave Chris full visitation rights, while providing that the children would be raised in the Jewish religion.

Chris's sister Michelle Harring, then a school principal in New York state, was one of the sharpest skeptics regarding what in 1983, when Danielle was born, seemed to most a certain-disaster scenario. As Chris recalls:

"During Danielle's early years, Michelle would call regularly to reprimand me and tell me I had done a terrible thing. According to her, my daughter was going to suffer intolerably from the social stigma of having gay parents. I'd tell her, 'Okay, I honor your opinion but I really don't believe that's the case. Let's see what happens." What happened, Chris says, is that by the time Avi came along, Michelle was "the first to admit that she was wrong." And Danielle now describes Michelle as "an incredibly loving and devoted aunt to both of us." Among other things, Danielle has accompanied Michelle and her husband Sidney on numerous vacation trips.

Chris acknowledges that differences sometimes arose in the early years because of his more disciplined approach to childrearing, a result of his French European heritage, but generally has always recognized the women's role as primary parents. And in the long run, he feels it was "enriching" for the kids to be exposed to the varying views and backgrounds.

Takoma Park is a small, neighborly town of about

nineteen thousand, essentially residential with only the barest of commercial districts, its narrow streets lined with multistory, turn-of-the-last-century frame houses shaded by towering oaks and elms. Now, same-sex parents are quite common—at least five such families live within a few blocks of the house where Danielle and Avi grew up. But when the kids were little, theirs was an oddity, and their mothers willfully shouldered the task of educating not only their children, but their neighbors, playmates, and other parents.

With Danielle's birth, Dana abandoned her career and became a stay-at-home mom for her daughter's first five years.

"We talk about math prodigies and chess prodigies," she laughs. "Well, Danielle is what I call a social prodigy. When she was two, doing something terrible-two-ish, and I yelled at her, she turned to me and said, 'Stop yelling at me. It's not good for me.'"

At Avi's birth, with Susan working long hours that often included nighttime meetings, Dana decided not to return to the career path she had earlier chosen, settling instead for a more routine job as a county social worker that would allow more flexibility to be on call for the kids.

The children themselves each realized early on that their family was different from that of many of their friends. (Susan remembers one of Danielle's little friends at a sleepover at their house saying to Danielle, "You have two moms. Did you come half out of one and half out of the other?") And the women always made clear that hiding the facts from others was just plain wrong—as Dana says, "Just as we would never stand for it if the children wanted to hide being Jewish." She adds:

"We were never closeted, never not open about the family and the children. I think people accepted it all before they realized they were accepting it. It's different when they meet real human beings than it is if you ask them in theory how they feel about such things."

So the women never attempted to explain themselves, but let the situation speak for itself. One mother later told them it had taken her an entire evening at a gathering of preschool parents, listening to Susan talk about *her* daughter and Dana talk about *her* daughter, before it finally clicked that they were talking about the same girl.

Art Thomas, the only African American in the variegated cast, remains in awe and gratitude at how open Susan and Dana were in their neighborhood. He recalls:

"If they were having some kids and their parents over, they always asked if I wanted to be included. And when I was introduced to the family friends, it was always, 'This is the kids' other dad.' There was never any hesitation about it. And I was amazed how many of the neighbors already knew who I was before I ever met them, because they had already heard about me. It was great to feel so welcome."

The mothers made certain, however, that the kids always knew there were other children in similar families. Susan was pregnant with Danielle less than a month when she and Dana helped form a group of like-minded lesbian mothers-to-be. They saw to it that at least some of their children's early playmates also had same-sex parents. And they carefully chose a preschool open to diversity: Among other things, it featured a unit on "The Family," which explained that some kids have only one parent, others have one parent at home and another living somewhere else, while others might have two mothers or two fathers at home.

The kids have always called Chris "Papa" and in their early years regularly spent weekends at his house, as Danielle puts it, "getting instructed in the art of train sets and lego architecture." Then, when Danielle was seven and Avi two, Chris partnered domestically with Art Thomas.

By the accounts of all, it was bonding at first sight between the children and Art. As Susan puts it (and Chris agrees), Art is "more domestic-focused" than Chris. When the kids were little and spent the weekend with them, it was generally Art who made the scrambled eggs and got them dressed in the morning.

Thus, despite their massive differences in background, and their late start at the parent-child game, the mutual fondness and dependence between the kids and Art remains clear in every smile, gesture or shared memory that passes among them.

Although he had never planned on having his own children, Art grew up in a large family, had always liked kids, and, in particular, was instantly more adept than Chris at handling a sometimes difficult two-year-old Avi. (Now, more than a decade later, Art and Avi regularly speak as a team before groups of wannabe gay fathers in Washington.)

After Art's arrival, Danielle and Avi stepped up the

frequency of their weekend stays at Chris's home. So it often became the Sunday morning duty of the white, Catholic-raised Chris and the black, Baptist-raised Art, to get the kids dressed, fed, and delivered on time to their Hebrew school.

Now, in Danielle's words, "Papa has been a huge part of our intellectual and cultural development, introducing us to much of the world through books and travel, while Art is the more day-to-day father." And Art says, "I think it's the greatest gift of my life, even though my relationship with Chris didn't work out."

Asked how he happened to bond with two children unrelated to him and whom he had not known from infancy, Art's shrug implies that he finds it a dumb question.

"Danielle and Avi were with us almost every weekend. When you spend a lot of time with kids and get to know what's important to them, you care about them. How can you help but?"

On a typical Saturday, he says, they'd read stories, play games, watch TV. "And cooking was always a big thing with Danielle. She liked to cook and bake and didn't really do a lot of that with her moms for some reason. So whenever I was cooking dinner, she'd help out. And then she'd want to bake something for her moms.

"It was kind of funny. With two moms, she'd be baking at our house."

When Chris and Art broke up after five years, the children's relationship with both men suffered nary a ripple. Even today, nearly a decade later, when talking with others, they invariably refer to Art as "our Dad," even though when they're with him, he's just plain "Art."

"At one point after we had broken up," Art says, "Susan and Dana asked if it was okay for the kids to call me 'Dad' since they refer to Chris as 'Papa.' But they had always called me 'Art.' We understand what our relationship is. To call me 'Dad' isn't necessary.

"I think of them as my kids, and that's all that matters—our relationship."

⤳

In the summer of 2001, ABC's *20/20* show featured Susan, Dana, Danielle, and Avi in a program devoted to children growing up in gay families. There, Barbara Walters made the obvious point that having gay parents forces children to confront antigay cultural attitudes. Walters suggested that perhaps Susan and Dana were being selfish—"that yes, you wanted to have children, but you've asked too much of your kids by forcing them to have to deal with society's attitude toward you as gay people." Susan's reply:

"If wanting to have children and then having a family together where the children . . . are doing well or are going to be really good people, if that's being selfish . . . I stand guilty."

The women are understandably skeptical about the proposition that children need both a male and female role model inside the home.

"I don't think it's the gender of a person that defines what they bring to parenthood," Susan says. "Someone who is gentle and easy going, or someone who is highly competitive, can be of either gender. As compared to a single parent, it's probably helpful to have two parents interacting in a loving household. But the idea that that has to be a man and a woman seems silly.

"And it's an odd assumption that you don't have men in the children's lives just because you don't have a husband. My father was a special, charismatic, lovely person who was very close to both the kids until his death a few years ago. My sisters' husbands are caring uncles, close to the kids.

"Life is richer than just who your spouse is. You can get a lot of contact with men just by day-to-day living."

Dana's father has also been consistently in the children's lives from birth, representing the family at Danielle's junior year Family Visiting Week at college.

And then, of course, there are the kids' two fathers and *their* large extended families. No one has bothered to tally the total number of cousins with whom Danielle and Avi are close. Susan's two sisters and their husbands, living in North Carolina, have nine children between them, and the three families generally get together anywhere from four to six times a year. Chris stems from a large French family, and Danielle and Avi have visited and taken trips with numerous of his scattered multitude of nieces, nephews, and cousins. (Danielle once spent most of a summer with Chris's mother and one of his cousins in Paris, and she returned home from her 2004 semester in Africa via a two-week Paris stopover visit with the same relatives.)

All of which can make for especially hectic holidays: "You really have to block out your time and schedule it to the minute to make sure you see everybody," Danielle says. Art laughs, "It helps that Christmas and Chanukah don't fall together."

On Christmas break of Danielle's junior year, she squeezed in a New York visit with aunts and uncles (Chris's brothers and sisters); celebrated Christmas with Susan, Dana, and Avi at the home of Art and Mark with Mark's parents also on hand; and observed Chanukah at Susan's, where Art and Mark joined a houseful of Susan's relatives who had driven up from North Carolina.

And it was a less busy holiday than usual because of the absence of Chris and his parents, who were vacationing in Mexico!

~

Dana's own answer to Barbara Walters's question about cultural bias bordered on the flippant: "I didn't worry about my children feeling comfortable with gay parents. I worried about my daughter being teased for having a fat mother."

In fact, of course, Dana's casual dismissal of the point masked the well-thought-out precautions taken by her and Susan to ease their children's way. Still, the mothers seemed somewhat surprised to learn from Walters's questioning of Danielle that their daughter had for a time in middle school actually felt ashamed of having lesbian mothers. Danielle "put on a happy face" at home, she told Walters, because she didn't want to hurt Susan and Dana. But the need to pretend only added another layer of shame:

"My parents were loving and I knew they would do anything for me, so I felt extremely guilty that I was acting ashamed of who they were."

In seventh grade, Danielle even refrained for months from telling her best friend Michelle Desimone, despite the fact that they were "inseparable at school" and spent hours on the telephone every night.

"I didn't invite Michelle to our house even though she continually invited me to hers," Danielle remembers. "It was a bad conflict because I really wanted her to meet my family and to be able to invite her. I knew her family was fairly conservative and I was terrified I might lose a friend.

"Then one night I finally got the courage to tell her and I was sobbing on the phone. 'I have to tell you something,' I said, and she thought I was dying or had done something really terrible."

Danielle laughs at the memory. "I told her my mothers were lesbian—and she actually knew! She said she had known since third grade!

"But there was a homophobic atmosphere during middle school. 'That's so gay' was a popular slur and being labeled a 'fag' was a common insult." She says she constantly heard "careless hate speech" that in effect derogated her own family.

On the *20/20* show Michelle said Danielle went from her "darkest time" of being "intensely secretive" to the friend she described as "popular . . . very extroverted . . . and most importantly, she's completely open."

For Danielle—as for hundreds of other children of same-sex parents in recent years—the key to full openness

was the annual Cape Cod Family Week staged by the
Family Pride Coalition (see chapter 2.) With Susan,
Dana and Avi, Danielle attended for the first time in the
summer of 1998, and it was a turning point in the lives
of both kids.

It was "amazing" Danielle says, to meet dozens of
other teenagers with parents and families like her own.
It opened "a whole new world" for her, helped erase any
fear of discrimination, and inspired her to educate the
mainstream about her family.

They've returned to the Cape every summer since, and
both Danielle and Avi have become extremely active
with the Family Pride offshoot known as COLAGE
(Children of Lesbians and Gays Everywhere), Danielle
as a member of the board.

At first, Susan discounted Danielle's *20/20* comments
about her middle school travails. Perhaps, she thought,
Danielle was merely echoing some of what she had
heard from others at COLAGE. During her middle
school years, Susan says, Danielle in fact was "always
popular" and had regular sleepovers and birthday parties at their house.

But Danielle is articulate and detailed in her memories. The friends at those sleepovers and birthday parties,
she says, were longtime family friends; they didn't
include any of her new friends in middle school because
she feared how they might react.

Such differences of perspective are common between
same-sex parents and their children during the growing-
up years, according to Abigail Garner, author of *Families
Like Mine*. Because they fear hurting them, she says,

what children tell their parents can be "really different from the reality they share in COLAGE." (see chapter 5.)

Although he was in middle school when the *20/20* show aired, Avi indicated to Walters that unlike his sister, he wasn't particularly concerned about classmates knowing his parents were gay. And now, in high school, his independent posture seems to render him immune to possible stigma. As I write, for example, he is the only non-gay member of the school's Gay Straight Alliance. A favorite activity is conducting diversity workshops at school. And he's been known to sport a T-shirt at school bearing the message, "Marriage Is a Human Right Not a Heterosexual Privilege."

Virtually every child growing up with same-sex parents has to confront the misguided notion that gay parents tends to "influence" their children to be gay. It is of course inevitable that some children of either straight or gay parents will be gay, but that the overwhelming proportion in either case will be straight.

Just as inevitable is the media's pressing curiosity about the matter of sexual orientation.

On the *20/20* show, in response to her direct question, Danielle told Barbara Walters that she's heterosexual. Off camera, Danielle laughs at the notion that the heterosexuality of a child of gay parents should be "news." On the same *20/20* show, Walters also interviewed Alex Tinker (see chapter 1), and Danielle asks drily, "How many shots did they have of him kissing his girl friend?"

More seriously, Danielle says that having gay parents and being part of a multiracial family has instilled in her a deep sense of responsibility to take on social justice causes. Art's role in her life has sharpened her sensitivity to the broader problems of diversity in general. In her earlier years, she says, the fact that Art is African American was sometimes as troublesome to her as having two mothers.

"At a school function or birthday party, I'd think, how do I explain it to other kids. I couldn't just say, 'This is my dad,' since he obviously wasn't my biological father. So then you get into the whole thing about having gay parents, too."

She "never would have objected" to Art attending such functions, but admits it sometimes made her uncomfortable: "When you are different from other people, you have to take that extra step to explain your situation and then leave yourself and your family vulnerable to bigotry. Sometimes you just don't want to explain your family."

If Art's being black can muddle the kids' friends, their own whiteness regularly creates even more confusion at his office.

On two occasions, Art has taken Avi to his office on a "take-your-child-to-work day," and he recalls:

"People would say, 'Oh, your son, which one is he?' I'd say, 'Here, he's right here. This is my son right here.' They'd pause, then say, 'Okay,' and just go on. They don't understand but just leave it at 'Okay.'"

Among his pictures at his office is one of Danielle and some friends on the occasion of their high school prom. One of the friends is Angie, who is black, and that can be another source of bafflement to visitors to Art's office. He laughs as he describes such an occasion:

"I'd say, 'This is my daughter's prom.' They'd say, 'Oh,

she looks great in that black dress.' And I'd say, 'Actually, my daughter is wearing red.'"

One colleague working on the Web with him one day noted a picture of his entire family on the bulletin board behind his desk, and said, "I've been meaning to ask, are you related to this guy?"

"He's my partner," Art replied.

"Well, who are those kids?" she asked.

"Those are my children."

"Well, uh, you and he, uh, uh . . ."

Such experiences have taught him that explaining all the details at the beginning of a conversation can save a lot of trouble.

Once, before he came to that bit of wisdom, he was talking with a new woman in the office and casually mentioned "my kids." She said, "Oh, you have kids?" He said, "Well, they're my ex's kids." And she asked, "Is she working here, too." He took a deep breath, pointed to the picture of the family, and replied:

"Well, listen, I'm gay, my ex is a man. These are his kids, and those are their mothers."

Danielle smiles knowingly at Art's stories: "A lot of the problem is vocabulary. When I try to explain Art's relationship to me, or Chris's relationship to me, there isn't a word for it. It requires a sentence or two."

Or three or four?

Parental breakups can create a broad range of effects on children. Sometimes, when the parents are genuinely committed to the priority of the children's welfare, the kids can actually be better off. They no longer hear the bickering, while knowing they're still loved by both parents. Those of course are not the split-ups we read about, but they are not uncommon, among either gay or straight parents.

Breakups between same-sex parents present an additional complication, since the nonbiological (or non-adoptive) parent under many circumstances can be legally excluded from visitation or custody rights.

In the case of Susan and Dana, for the first years of their children's lives, Dana's legal status was even more tenuous than that of most nonbiological gay parents, where the donor typically is either unknown or someone who never planned to be an active father in any event. In 1998, she applied for second-parent adoption, asking the court to validate her as the children's third parent. The judge found that adoption would be "in the best interests of these children," since "by all accounts the children have flourished under their [i.e. Susan's and Dana's] care." The judge refused, however, to recognize all three parents in the absence of legal precedent, and Susan scoured the law books in vain for even a single appellate court decision that fit their situation. Accordingly, as a condition of approving adoption by Dana, the court required Chris to terminate his parental status, while retaining his legal rights to access and visitation.

Both Chris and Dana acknowledge that the court proceeding was difficult for them. They had often had areas of important personal differences, but always managed a healthy working relationship where the children were concerned. And when push came to shove, Chris says, "It didn't make sense for me to be dictatorial and say I'm the father and to hell with you." Dana's relationship to the kids, he says, reminds him of his own governess as a child: "Always present, totally preoccupied if they had a little sniffle or whatever, Dana was there."

So the law no longer recognizes Chris as the children's father, which of course is of no moment whatever to Danielle and Avi, to whom he remains their fond "Papa."

Meanwhile, long before she and Susan ended their relationship, Dana's devotion as a mother led her to move out of Takoma Park to nearby Bethesda. Avi was having learning difficulties stemming from an attention deficit problem, and the search for help had led to a Bethesda school with a teacher especially skilled with gifted children. So Dana moved, solely to qualify Avi for attendance there, and has continued to live in the same house since breaking up with Susan.

Avi divided his time between the two houses until he started high school in Silver Spring, adjacent to Takoma Park, where the demands have kept him from spending as much time as before with Dana. But they talk on the telephone, literally every day, and he spends weekends with her.

Both Chris and Art frequently have dinner at Dana's or Susan's house. Dana feels especially close to Art: "If I need someone to help me, I know I can always count on Art. He's like a brother who is always there for you." As to her split with Susan, Dana observes:

"I think why our children got through it relatively

unscathed, unlike a lot of children in divorce, is that they had already seen Chris and Art break up. And they could say, 'But they're still our dads, and they're still friends.'

"Our kids can honestly say they have four parents."

8.

The "Gastro-Evangelist" and the Church of the Future

R everend Bill Frank is a retired Congregationalist
minister who chaired the search committee that
chose Andrew Warner over forty-two other candidates to
become a minister at Milwaukee's Plymouth United
Church of Christ. He says Andrew has been, as it were,
a Godsend to the church: "He has a way of attracting
people who need the church and finding a way to fit
them in."

When he interviewed for the Plymouth post, Andrew
knew the search committee wasn't concerned about his
sexual orientation, since approximately 20 percent of the

congregation was gay or lesbian. Nevertheless, as he recalls:

"I sensed they were a little nervous about my partner Jay. They didn't know if they were going to get RuPaul or someone like that. So they were relieved to find out he was an engineer."

Andrew and Jay Edmundson formalized their commitment in a June 18, 2000, Holy Union at Plymouth, officiated by Martin Smith, one of Andrew's seminary friends, then an Episcopal abbot, now a priest. They chose that day because of what they call an "auspicious alignment" of dates: it was Trinity Sunday on the church calendar, Father's Day on the secular calendar. A standing-room-only crowd included most of the congregation, the parents of both, and numerous family members and friends—the latter including a Lutheran and a Congregationalist minister, both friends from Andrew's seminary days.

As it turned out, it was just a few weeks later that the men became fathers, with the arrival of their first son, Tomas, age seven months. "There were a lot of bad jokes about it being a shotgun wedding," Andrew laughs.

Andrew's sermons inevitably reflect his deeply committed biblical grounding. But they often reflect as well his equally profound commitment to his family—his partner Jay, a former Naval submarine officer who is now a commercial engineer, and the men's lively, outgoing Guatemalan-born adopted sons, Tomas and David.

Plymouth Church was founded in 1841 and its current English Gothic edifice, erected in 1913 in a stately neighborhood one block east of the local campus of the

University of Wisconsin, bears all the hallmarks of its devout Congregationalist tradition. From the pulpit, Andrew and Senior Minister Mary Ann Neevel look out over the congregation and choir loft to a majestic Tiffany stained glass window depicting Sophia, Angel of Wisdom, which prompts Andrew to observe, "Clergy have the best view in the house."

Another, more mundane, of Plymouth's attractions to Andrew—an avid chef who sometimes describes himself as a "gastro-evangelist"—is the fact that the church has a kitchen on each of its three floors.

The congregation of three-hundred-plus members called Andrew when he was just twenty-five and a recent graduate of Harvard Divinity School. Now, eight years later, he is an increasingly popular dispenser of traditional Christianity. "He's a fine minister, a wonderful pastor, and he's becoming a really *great* preacher," says longtime Plymouth member Dor Rohlfing, who with husband David raised three now-grown children with the aid of the church.

Still, the search committee chair himself has a few misgivings. For one thing, Bill Frank is a product of Yale Divinity School, Harvard's natural rival. (Says a smiling Frank, "The rest of the committee was impressed with his Harvard education, I wasn't. . . . I tell Andrew my classmates were his professors.") For another, Andrew is tad *too* traditional for Frank's own less literalist theological tastes.

Thus, while agreeing wholeheartedly with the core message of a recent Warner sermon—the importance of "[devoting] ourselves in love to Jesus"—Frank would nonetheless be tempted to quibble with Andrew's seemingly literal reading of such Scripture passages as those telling of the raising of Lazarus from the dead, or of Jesus feeding five thousand people with two fishes and five loaves.

But no one in the congregation, including Frank, has the slightest problem with Andrew's sexual orientation. Six months after his arrival, Tomas was one of two sons of gay couples baptized at the same Sunday service. "So there were two boys and four fathers," Reverend Frank says. And as to that unusual cast of characters, he adds in something less than ministerial prose, "No one gave a damn."

David arrived two and a half years later, on December 20, 2002—just in time to fill the Baby Jesus role in that year's annual Christmas pageant. Unfortunately, David cried persistently, and an amused congregation stifled its laughter as a teenager cast as one of the kings rushed to the rescue with a milk bottle for "Mary" to give to "Jesus." (On behalf of his son, Andrew says, "It beats myrrh any day.")

While the church recognizes the union of Andrew and Jay, the state, of course, does not. So Andrew is not legally a father at all—Jay is formally the adopting parent and Wisconsin, unlike several other states, provides no option for "second-parent adoption." They have consulted a lawyer about the possibility of some other legal tie to the boys for Andrew, such as guardianship. Meanwhile, an adoring father-in-fact is eternally grateful to congregants whose personal Christian faith couldn't care less about mundane legalities.

⁓

Plymouth United Church of Christ has a long and honored tradition of social gospel in its heavily ethnic heartland industrial city. Before the turn of the twentieth century, the church devoted an entire building, complete with a gym, library, and little theater, to serving the needy in the heart of downtown Milwaukee. It was instrumental in the founding of a boys club and YMCA, and sponsored a lecture series that filled its eight-hundred-seat auditorium for visiting speakers from all over the country.

That heritage continues to infuse the church in its current North Shore setting and has lured a number of retired ministers to the congregation—at one point, no fewer than fifteen at the same time. The church is on record as having a "dream of a multiracial, multi-ethnic, and just congregation and community." It regularly supplies volunteers to an inner city ministry, Habitat for Humanity, and an organization serving the elderly. In 2001, it sponsored and resettled a refugee family from Burma. At Sunday service, you can occasionally spot a homeless person, perhaps with some severely disabling condition. "That's the way a church ought to be . . . how wonderful we have a church that's really open," Frank says.

In the Plymouth spirit, Frank's theological differences with Andrew are essentially beside the point. What *is* important, he says, is that Andrew "is just a super person trying to walk in the ways of Jesus." Andrew himself underscored the secondary significance of doctrine in a sermon in words that now grace the church website: "We do not have any one creed that mandates what we ought to believe. What unites us is a common commitment to love God and love our neighbors in ways which reflect the life and teachings of Jesus Christ."

Now, in its casual welcoming of lesbians and gay men, its unselfconscious mix of straight and gay, Plymouth is perhaps a prototype of the American church of the future. Gay and lesbian congregants are fully active, for example, in committee leadership and participation in its extensive music program that includes three choirs and a concert chorale. They're part of a "Bon Appetit" program of eight-person groups in which members rotate as hosts of pot luck suppers. And the current church moderator, in effect the president of the congregation, is Britt Brown, a gay man. (Britt, with partner Noel Rosado, happens also to be a father of an adopted African American boy who shared that baptism with Tomas and who now calls Tomas "my best friend.")

Plymouth is one of a significant number of UCC churches that have voted to expressly designate themselves as "open and affirming" to sexual minorities. Pastor Neevel and Bill Frank initiated the process in the late 1980s via a series of lively after-church discussions that produced a number of unexpected revelations. One member disclosed that his twin brother was a gay man running a repertoire theater in Germany. A woman said, "I think my mother is a lesbian." And one man, whom many had always thought of as homophobic, himself came out as gay after the "open and affirming" vote.

⁓

Tomas is a round-faced, bright-eyed youngster with dark hair and brown eyes, an extremely physical child with, in the words of his "Nana" (Andrew's mother), "just nothing that he doesn't greet as a challenge." In his fathers' comfortable Whitefish Bay home two miles north of Plymouth Church, his first word was "ball." By age two, an apparent natural athlete, he was swinging a big yellow bat at balls thrown by either "Papa" (Jay) or "Daddy" (Andrew), and by the time he was three, he was an avid fan of both the Whitefish Bay High School Blue Dukes and Milwaukee Brewers baseball teams. "See my Brewers shirt!" he commands a visitor, pointing to a picture of himself proudly sporting a miniature version of the major league team uniform.

David is also dark-haired and brown-eyed, less exuberant and physical in nature than Tomas, with fine, almost angelic features, and a loving disposition. His warm grin and winning manner helped him merge quickly into his Milwaukee family with—at least for the first few years—minimum display of sibling jealousy from Tomas.

The family scrapbooks include pictures of both boys' mothers. Tomas's mother was an eighteen-year-old single Guatemalan woman who became homeless when her father threw her out of their house because she was pregnant. David's mother, shortly before his birth, left an abusive relationship to become an indentured servant and felt unable to handle him.

Because of Andrew's relationship to Plymouth Church, the boys' immediate world is perhaps significantly larger and more filled with playmates and caring adults than that of most children. Aside from the usual complement of neighbors and family friends, Tomas and David are especially cherished by the Plymouth congregation. Dor and David Rohlfing, for example, consider the two dads and their boys "kind of an extension of our family," and they see each other frequently though they live four miles apart.

Even before Jay left for Guatemala to pick up Tomas, several church members had scheduled baby showers for the dads-to-be. Dor hosted one of the showers—which, because Jay was able to pick up Tomas earlier than originally planned, actually took place after his arrival. At her shower, Dor composed a special song dedicated to the new parents. And Reverend Neevel, a married mother of two, was one of several friends who drove to their house to unload gifts of toys.

Every week day other than Wednesday (his day off) Andrew simply takes the boys to work with him, since their day care center, although run by an independent organization, is physically located at Plymouth Church. Many of their playmates there are also children of church members. Andrew spends Wednesdays at home with the boys. But on other week days, since they're handy at the church, he's also able to see them often during working hours, sometimes for lunch.

The boys will find themselves unusual neither for being adopted nor having same-sex parents. A number of other congregation couples, including some who are gay and lesbian, also have adopted children.

The Warner-Edmundson clan's relations with two of

the Plymouth families—the Clancys and the Draper-
Rasts—demonstrate the kind the kind of close-knit ties
that Andrew's church role has made possible with so
many of his congregants.

John Clancy is a member of a men's group with
Andrew, his wife Christi is part of a cooking group that
Andrew helped form, and Tomas is a playmate of the
Clancy's son Tim. Christi calls Andrew "an amazing
chef" and says Tomas "has this incredible arm" with a
baseball. Weather permitting, play dates arranged by the
parents for Tomas and Tim ordinarily end up in a front-
yard T-ball game.

Cliona Draper and her husband Joel Rast are now
members of the church, but they first met Andrew at a
neighborhood park where their children were playing
together. When Cliona asked Andrew if he was a stay-at-
home father, she learned both that he was a minister and
had a gay partner. Now, her daughter is in the church
day care program and continues to play with Tomas
there, while Cliona appreciates Andrew not only as a
father but as pastor: "He's very down to earth, very good
at connecting."

Then there is the boys' extended family, which
includes four doting grandparents. "We're very blessed,"
Jay says. "We have two sets of parents who bend over
backwards taking care of us, worrying about us, taking
care of our kids."

Andrew's mother Barbara says of Tomas and David: "I
just adore them. I didn't realize how quickly I could lose
my heart to children who are adopted. . . . I'd give them
the world." Indeed, Barbara is so taken that she and her

husband Tom have invested in a condo near the church
so she can be with the boys and their dads approximately
four months each year. Milwaukee is just two hours
flying time from their home in Northern Virginia, and
Barbara is often accompanied by Grandpa Tom,
although his visits are usually limited by business pressures to three or four days.

The Warners say they are probably closer to the two
boys than they were to any of their earlier seven grandchildren, probably because of the difficult background
circumstances that brought Tomas and David to the
family:

"My heart goes out to these two in a special different
way," Barbara says. "And they've been so open and
receptive, it's wonderful to hear their voices say, 'Nana,
Nana.'"

Ironically, though, both of the now-doting grandmothers were initially somewhat taken aback—and had to
be set right by Jay's father, a retired Navy commander—
when they learned that their sons intended to become
fathers. While the two men were waiting for Tomas,
Jay's parents, Jean and Jim Edmundson, drove from their
Sarasota, Florida, home to visit the Warners in Northern
Virginia. As they discussed the new development, Barbara revealed her rather conventional misgivings.

"I said, 'Children need mothers,' and I said I didn't
know how it was going to be for this baby to have two
fathers." To which Jim Edmundson replied:

"Well, I just want to say at a time in life when we
thought we knew it all, our kids taught us that we
didn't. I'm looking forward to the next lesson. I'm

looking forward to pushing that baby carriage and getting to know this baby."

As Barbara now sees it, looking back: "It's one thing to have homophobia, but now I had some sexism going on. I worried at first that maybe Andy and Jay wouldn't know what to do.

"Well, sometimes they don't know what to do, but I didn't always know what to do either when I was a new mother.

"I just had to get over that ugly sexist attitude. I've come to realize that these little boys couldn't be loved or cared for more than they are."

The two sets of grandparents visit and telephone frequently and they have planned overlapping stays as they did for David's baptism the Sunday after Easter. But Jay's mother now has difficulty flying, so the dads and boys have flown to Florida for several visits.

⁓

Long before David arrived, as Tomas grew out of the toddler stage, he launched the process that would vastly alter his fathers' lifestyle, the makeup of their circle of closest friends, their neighborhood relations—and, not unimportantly, their lifelong joint aversion to baseball.

Before becoming parents, many of their closest friends were childless gays and lesbians. Now they increasingly find themselves drawn to other parents, straight *and* gay, whether they be neighbors, fellow church members, or friends from other facets of their lives.

Most of Jay's friends from his Navy days, for example,

are now fathers, and every summer, Jay, Andrew and the boys travel to coastal Maine for a lobster and clambake reunion of submarine crew members and their families, hosted by Charlie Pendleton and his wife. Charlie is a close friend who worked under Jay both as an enlisted man in the sub's engine room and at the engineering firm in Minneapolis. He's one of no fewer than five former enlisted men at the annual get-together whom Jay later hired in civilian jobs.

At home, Tomas has been the catalyst for a number of friendships with neighbors—including one couple who at first didn't know how to deal with the unusual family across the street. And much of it happened because of Tomas' natural athletic skill and special love of baseball.

Even before speaking his first word, "ball," or able to stand and throw, Tomas' favorite activity was rolling a ball back and forth with another person. Virtually as soon as he could walk, he could throw. So like it or not— which they initially did not—Papa and Daddy found themselves in the front yard tossing a baseball with him. Often they were joined by Aaron Kessler, Tomas' best friend from down the street, and by Aaron's father and mother. Soon, front yard T-ball games became a popular neighborhood-wide attraction, complete with a cheering section of parents, many in portable chairs.

But across the street, for some weeks, Sam and his little brother Zack could only watch while walking up and down the other side of the street. Their parents, confused, confided in Aaron's parents that they didn't know how to explain to their sons why Tomas had two fathers and no mother. What did the Kesslers tell Aaron about this, they wanted to know. Aaron's mother's reply: "Oh, I just tell him they're two gay men."

Soon Sam and Zack were regular members of the game, and first his father Lou and then his mother Sharon joined the adult cheering section. The boys and their parents also became regular members of a neighborhood group at the games of the Whitefish Bay High School Blue Dukes ("Aaron and Tomas just go crazy at their games," Jay says), and occasionally those of the major league Brewers.

When David arrived, Sharon, by then quite comfortable with the dads across the street, brought a gift. And in 2003 when Jay and Andrew bought a new house a few blocks away, Sharon and Lou cared for Tomas during two of the days the fathers spent moving.

As they were toting their things into their new house, Andrew and Jay noticed a woman across the street looking at them quizzically. Eventually, she crossed over to inquire tentatively, "Aren't you the guys who go to the high school baseball games?" When they said they were, she ran back to her house and returned with a copy of the Blue Dukes baseball yearbook—which included pictures of two of the Dukes' most rabid fans, Aaron and Tomas! The woman's son, it turned out, was the Dukes' varsity catcher.

One spring afternoon when David was nearly two and Tomas four and a half, my wife and I arrived to find Andrew playing catch with Tomas in the front yard, with David tugging at Daddy's pants. Tomas reluctantly agreed to go inside, where Andrew gave the visitors a tour of the attractive four-bedroom neo-English Gothic house. The tour ended in a capacious playroom that had been built for the twelve children of a previous owner, but was now being quite adequately utilized, thank you, by its just two occupants, playing noisily among a mélange of toys and miniature furniture.

Suddenly, hearing the sound of a car driving into the detached garage, the boys abruptly deserted Daddy and his guests, deftly sidestepped the clutter on the floor, and raced to the side door screaming "Papa, Papa!" Moments later, Papa entered, grinning broadly, somehow simultaneously managing to hold, hug, and kiss two squirming boys in his arms.

It was a simple, everyday domestic scene—but one, the polls tell us, that would infuriate much of Middle America.

If their being gay seems now to be just one effortlessly integrated facet of an urbane lifestyle, earlier that was far from the case for either Andrew or Jay.

For Andrew, who came out to himself and his family at age nineteen, the journey to self-awareness was strewn with emotional land mines stemming in part from his deep religious faith. He now laughs as he recalls one ironic episode as an undergraduate at Colgate University, where he discovered his passion for religion courses, and where a nun at a campus retreat facility taught him to pray the rosary:

"So I'd do my fifty Hail Mary's praying that God would make me straight. Well, gay men used to refer to each other as 'Mary,' and here I was praying, 'Hail Mary.'"

Jay, by contrast, managed to avoid the reality of his sexuality until he was in his thirties. For him, it was a matter of "out of sight, out of mind"—a concerted focus on hard work and hard play to avoid acknowledging unwanted visions poking at the surface of his consciousness.

In a few respects, their growing up years were similar. Each was the youngest child in a large family, an Eagle Scout, an "A" student, and a well-liked teen whose relationships with girls tended to end in close friendships rather than romance. But in important ways, their early lives could not have been more different. Growing up, Andrew knew but a single home, in Reston, Virginia, a suburb of Washington, D.C., where his parents still live. By contrast, Jay's father was a career Navy officer, so Jay says he "grew up all over," including Hawaii, New Mexico, Pennsylvania, Florida, and Indiana.

In college, Andrew majored in religion, Jay in engineering. And that contrast in their chosen areas of study might stand as a sort of metaphor for their quite different personalities.

Andrew is tall, darkly handsome, ever thoughtful and warm, careful to find the right word or phrase, quick to smile or ad lib a joke, his keen sense of humor nevertheless failing to mask a deep introspective quality. Jay, shorter and sandy-haired, is Mister Spontaneity himself, with a seemingly easy outgoing manner that produces a steady flow of good-natured wit.

And those contrasting personalities, in turn, reflect the very different paths that ended in their chance meeting in Minneapolis, Minnesota in the fall of 1996.

When Barbara says, "Andrew always seemed like a gift," it could perhaps be written off as just another typical comment of a doting mother. Still, his childhood reflects some seemingly precocious qualities that foreshadow his special traits as an adult and help explain his mother's wonderment.

Most surprising to his parents was his early, essentially spiritual insight into human nature. When he was no more than four or five, the dinner conversation turned one night to some friends who were concerned that one of their daughters was not as pretty as her two sisters. "It's not what's on the outside that's important about a person," little Andy contributed. "It's what's on the inside."

And even as a youngster, he seemed to practice what he was preaching. "He's just never been one to see color, or age or ethnicity," Barbara says.

When he was twelve, his parents attended a gathering in the school auditorium for parents of two seventh grade home room classes. One of the teachers was black, the other white. Tom and Barbara approached the white teacher on the assumption that Andrew would have mentioned it if his teacher was black. "No," they were told, "Andy's in the other class."

Scouting was Andrew's principal interest throughout his school years, and it was his first scout campout that triggered what would become a lifelong passion with cooking. Turned off by the instant oatmeal the troop had for breakfast, he announced that from then on, *he* would cook the campout meals. Within a short time, his father says, the troop became known as "the gourmet patrol."

For the first seven years of his life, Andrew attended a Disciples of Christ church, the religion in which his father had grown up. Then, his parents joined the Catholic church. Both Andrew and his next older brother Robert were baptized there and grew up active and involved Catholics.

In retrospect, like so many gay and lesbian people, he says he felt "different" from others as a child. As an adolescent, he came to fear some flaw deep in his soul. Spurred by the words of the Catholic communion liturgy—"Only say the word and thou shalt be healed"—he prayed each night for healing.

"I didn't say what I wanted to be healed of, but it was essentially gay thoughts. I would be aware I thought so-and-so was 'cute' and fantasize about him, and I felt I *knew* that was wrong."

As an undergraduate at Colgate University, he joined and became quite active with a fraternity—on the theory, now amusing to him in its seriously flawed simplicity, that "living with this heterosexual group of guys would help me get straight." In fact, the fraternity's profound homophobia and sexism simply compounded his confusion.

Still refusing to say the word "gay" to himself, he sat alone in the chapel one day, feeling desolate.

"I just didn't have anything left to give to God, I didn't have any more prayers to say, I was just empty. And in that moment the Scriptures came to me." He thought of Jeremiah 1:4:

"It talks about how before you were born, 'I formed you in the womb, I named you before you were even born, I pointed you to be a prophet to the nation.' And I had a sense of God having a hand in making me gay.

"So I was able to both say I'm gay but also that God made me that way. I felt a real sense of blessing, reaffirmation. It was a powerful time of prayer. And things happened quickly from that time on."

He came out to close friends, including a few in the fraternity. But soon, in disgust at the continuing rampant homophobia of his "brothers," he deactivated. The fraternity's response was harsh. His ex-brothers refused to speak to him. Men who had been his friends now referred to him as dead and cut him out of their pictures.

It was a painful period but he managed to form a new group of friends. And largely through his reading of the theologians H. Richard Niebuhr and his more famous older brother Reinhold Niebuhr, whose first pastoral post was with a UCC church in Detroit, he became interested in the United Church of Christ.

So at Harvard Divinity School, one of the first things he did was to look into the UCC, and he liked what he found. After a period of soul-searching, during which he seriously considered remaining in the Catholic Church as an "agent of change," he left that church and joined the UCC. There, he says, "I could have a moral vision for life that made sense to me."

And importantly, he learned that a significant proportion of local UCC congregations were formally "open and affirming" churches that blessed same-sex unions and had no bars against hiring gay or lesbian ministers.

From Harvard, he enrolled in a residency program for ministers in Minneapolis, Minnesota. There, he would meet, and court, an engineer with a local firm named Jay Edmundson, who had only recently admitted to himself that he, too, was gay.

⁓

Jay's first thirty-some years revealed no hint—either to others or to himself, as he tells it—of the lurking non-conformist within. Rather, it traced a conventionally macho path from Eagle Scout to nuclear engineer to Naval submarine officer to civilian executive engineer.

The locale that comes closest to something Jay can call a "hometown" is a Crane, Indiana, naval station, where he attended eighth through eleventh grades. It was a one hundred square mile base, tightly guarded because of its highly secret ammunition research. But he and his family lived on a large lake with two boats and ample acreage nearby for hunting and "running with the dogs." To Jay, an avid Eagle Scout, it added up to "the great outdoors . . . my own playground."

Unfortunately for him, the family had to move when his father retired at the end of Jay's eleventh grade year, and they settled in Sarasota, Florida, where his parents still live. There, as a high school senior, Jay suffered all the indignities of an unwanted newcomer. He was refused admission to the National Honor Society because he hadn't been in the school for two years, was placed in remedial classes on the unwarranted parochial notion that his Indiana education necessarily was inadequate, and was placed as the band's third-chair trumpet while being refused the right, as a newcomer, to compete for first chair.

Recalling that frustrating year caused by his family's forced move, he resolves, "We'll never do that to our sons."

He returned to Indiana as soon as possible, to Purdue University, where he earned his engineering degree while serving with the Naval ROTC program. The program led to a five-year service commitment, which Jay remembers with extreme fondness. As an officer on a nuclear submarine, he rose in rank from ensign to full lieutenant, proud of himself and his cohorts as ranking among what he describes as the top 1 percent of Navy personnel.

Jay himself won a number of awards, one of them as the outstanding junior officer in the squadron fleet. One of the unofficial honors ("although it didn't *feel* like an honor") was being assigned to the helm during the most dangerous night-hours shift, so that the captain could feel comfortable enough to sleep, relatively assured of not being disturbed. Jay proudly recalls that the only time he called the captain—at 4 AM, in heavy harbor traffic, under storm conditions, with the radar out—the captain "was there in seconds, in his underwear" because, the captain would later tell him, "if you call me, I know there's something wrong."

For Jay, though, one the most gratifying aspects of submarine duty was simply that it kept him at sea as much as nine months a year and always inordinately busy and working hard. It was his personal "don't ask, don't tell" policy, immersing himself in a life that allowed him to set aside any thoughts of serious dating and, for the most part, the pesky homosexual feelings that sometimes edged into near-awareness.

"Coming out of the Navy, I knew I wasn't heterosexual but I still didn't want to deal with it," he says. So, though out of the service, he in effect set about replicating the demands the Navy had put on him. He took a job in the civilian nuclear industry in Connecticut, simultaneously enrolled in an engineering master's program, and filled in any spare time with skiing and other strenuous pastimes.

It was only after moving to a Minneapolis engineering firm in 1995 that he finally accepted the fact that he was gay and began attending the local Metropolitan Community Church, a worldwide fellowship of Christian churches with predominantly gay congregations. There, one Sunday, although unknown to him at the time, he was spotted by a guest at the church who instantly found him attractive. The guest, no surprise here, was Andrew Warner.

⁓

Accompanying a friend to the MCC Sunday service, Andrew noticed "this cute guy a couple of pews ahead." Andrew looked for him at coffee hour, but he wasn't there. At coffee, though, Andrew did meet some members of a gay and lesbian camping group and accepted their invitation to join them on a campout the following weekend. And there, to his delight, he was introduced to another member of the group, the "cute guy" from the prior Sunday, Jay Edmundson.

Jay sums up their courtship in four words: "Luckily, Andrew is outgoing." And they agree that the crucial step in their relationship came when Andrew called Jay to invite him to a dinner party on the coming Friday night.

"Actually, I didn't even have a dinner party planned," Andrew says. "But he said he'd come, so I called everyone I'd met in the last three weeks and had them over for dinner."

Here, Andrew displays his pride in his culinary mastery: "I think after he tasted my cooking, he decided he was gong to stick around."

Whatever the lure, the attraction quickly proved mutual. They were soon living together, and less than a year later Andrew got the call to Plymouth Church. Fortunately, Jay was coincidentally tiring of his current job's travel demands, and was able to find an appealing new one in the Milwaukee area. In September of 1997, the couple moved to a house near the church, later moving a few miles away, after their sons' arrival, to Whitefish Bay on the city's northern edge.

It was only after settling down with Andrew that Jay told his parents he was gay. He says they had no special problem with that, and he attributes his father's easy acceptance to the fact that the former Navy commander was so accustomed to giving orders: "He just issued a new order, 'It's okay to have a gay son.'"

Jay says he has "always been good with kids," and assumed he could be a good father, but he had put the notion out of his mind when he accepted the fact that he was gay. For Andrew, however, the fatherhood instinct was always an uppermost passion. Then one evening during dinner at the home of church members Libby and Eddy Greaves, Libby asked Andrew what had been his biggest disappointment in life. Andrew told her it was that being gay meant he would never be a father. "That's crazy," Libby said. "You can adopt."

The rest, as it were, is history. With another gay couple in the church, Britt Brown and Noel Rosado, Andrew formed a "maybe baby" group of about eight gay and lesbian couples interested in having children. They explored and discussed the various available options, such as adoption, artificial insemination, surrogate mothering and in vitro conception. "Maybe baby" was a hugely successful operation: Today, its members have some eleven children. One pair of gay dads even have triplets—born to a surrogate mother.

Andrew and Jay found the adoption process itself relatively smooth and simple, except for the "ton of paperwork." They accomplished it through a Seattle agency that works with agencies in Russia and China as well as Guatemala, and chose the latter because of their own feelings of attachment to Hispanic culture. The Seattle agent knew they were gay, but when Jay picked up Tomas, no one in the Guatemalan agency ever asked him about a wife, much less about sexual orientation. "They knew what was happening," he believes, but says they pursue a 'don't ask, don't tell' policy in the interest of the children: "They know the kids are going to good homes and will be much better off in this country."

Four years later, in a sermon on the transforming power of love and openness, Andrew asked the congregation to consider the ways in which Plymouth had been "transformative to your life."

In his own case, he said, "I can't imagine a better place to raise my boys because I know this community cares for us." He thanked the member of the church who inspired Jay and him to work a day a month building and repairing homes for the poor with Habitat for Humanity.

"And frankly," he added, "it was a member of our church who once told us we could adopt. Recalling that evening at the Greaves, he said, "I had never imagined it. . . .They called us to try adoption, and I'm so thankful they did."

⁓

In February of 2003, House Majority Leader Tom DeLay of Texas, an outspoken cultural conservative, went on national television and co-wrote a *USA Today* opinion piece (with New York Senator Hillary Rodham Clinton, no less!) deploring the condition of the nation's homeless children. America needs to build a system, he explained to CNN's Judy Woodruff, that gives such children "a stable home" and insures that "they're raised by people that truly love them and want to see them succeed."

A year later DeLay would be among the first to voice his indignation at the approval of gay marriage in the state of Massachusetts. Congress, he told the *Boston*

Globe, should do "whatever it takes" to derail same-sex unions.

As one concerned about the state of homeless children, one is led to wonder what DeLay might have to say about the story of Tomas and David (or of the foster children of Steven Lofton and Roger Croteau, in chapter 6.)

In late 2002, when Jay Edmundson flew to Guatemala for a second time to pick up David, he sat next to a Guatemalan businessman and his wife, accompanied by two obviously non-Hispanic children. The couple explained that they had adopted the children in Europe— that they were fearful of adopting in their own country because they were well off, and the birth mother might "come and beg and cause us a lot of heartache." That told Jay all he needed to know about the odds of Tomas or David finding adoptive parents capable of truly caring for them in their home country.

He thought about that as he drove through the Guatemalan countryside, past "shanty housing going on for miles and miles," reflecting on the huge disparity between the country's wealthy and the poor. And an exclamation point was added at virtually every stop light, where hordes of little boys besieged his car, their hands out, begging for coins. "Some of them were no older than Tomas and some even looked like Tomas," he recalls. "It was just scary."

That's one reason the dads are not overly concerned about problems that might confront the boys because of having same-sex parents.

"Sure, they'll face things in intermediate and high school that won't be great," Andrew concedes.

He says his parents told him that people shouldn't have children unless they think there is some unique gift they have to give. "As I thought about adoption, I thought well, the bar is a little different than having birth children. So when we were talking about it, I thought we had a real gift we could give to our boys. However difficult it is for them in intermediate or high school, it's far better than what they would have had otherwise."

Besides, he adds, no one should grow up in a cocoon, protected from life's often harsh realities. He recalls the story of the Buddha, who grew up in a highly protected environment, shielded from any hint of pain or want, but who only began his path to enlightenment when he ventured into the world and witnessed poverty, sickness, and death.

As Andrew spoke, the boys ran into the room to show some visitors a pair of paper cutout birds they had attached to a stick in a manner that would allow the birds to appear to be flying. Andrew explained that earlier in the day, they had been very upset when a bird had killed itself by flying into the glass window of their playroom. Andrew and Jay helped them bury the bird, conduct a funeral, and cut out the paper birds in their memory.

"We talked to them about death," Andrew said. "We don't want them in the cocoon that so many Americans grow up in. So when they face bigotry, we'll talk to them about bigotry. Instead of protecting them along the way, we want to show them what we think is a more enlightened way to live.

"But that isn't pretending there isn't going to be diffi-culty. We just don't want them living in fear—it's going to ruin their lives."

⁓

In 2004, when gay marriage emerged as a key national political issue, it spawned a spate of state legislation throughout the country aimed at banning same-sex marriage. In Wisconsin, the proposed state constitu-tional ban took a particularly harsh form, outlawing not only gay marriage but gay civil unions as well, and phrased in a manner that could be interpreted as barring any sort of legal benefit whatever—domestic partner-ship or health benefits, for example—for same-sex cou-ples. (After limiting marriage to a union between a man and a woman, its second sentence provided that "A legal status identical or substantially similar to that of mar-riage for unmarried individuals shall not be valid or rec-ognized in this state.")

On Lincoln's Birthday, 2004, Andrew testified against the amendment before the Judiciary Committee of the State Assembly. The hearing room environment was wholly unreceptive, the amendment sponsor caustic in his remarks to the gays and lesbians present, while treating his own supporters with gracious courtesy. Andrew, nervous from the start, felt the hatred prompted by his own testimony and "it shook me up."

He opened by observing that Plymouth Church is one of the oldest Christian institutions in the state and that it had, "after prayerful consideration," been celebrating and blessing same-sex relationships for fifteen years. He noted that his church is hardly alone, but that people of faith from many Christian denominations similarly give their blessing to gay men and lesbians in committed relationships. And he described his own union with Jay, blessed by an Episcopal abbot and participated in as well by a Lutheran pastor and Congregational minister.

Hence, he asked, how could it be "right and proper for the Assembly to take a position on a matter of internal Christian debate." Such debates ought to take place "within Christianity, and among Christians," he said. The proposed amendment, he said, made no more sense than would one codifying into law the Roman Catholic position on a divorcee remarrying or the refusal of some churches to recognize interfaith marriage.

Then he talked movingly—before the hostile stares of obviously unmoved politicians—about his boys and other children in his church.

"I also come to you as a father, for I have two young sons—Tomas and David. In my congregation there are many like them—Bec, Sam, Olivia, Nicholas, Alison, Sage, Ian, Lucas, Simon, Ella, and, of course, baby Sienna who played Jesus in our Christmas pageant. The families of all of these children will be affected by the scope of this amendment. . . .

"It is difficult raising children without the legal protections and everyday assurances that come with marriage or civil unions. Last month, my eighteen month old baby, David, developed a breathing problem. His doctor told me to take him in to the emergency room; I rushed there with great concern for David. And when I drove up,

I panicked; what if they denied him treatment because I am not his legal father, or what if they didn't let me speak about his care because I'm not his legal father. No parent, and no child, should need to fear like that. What compelling state interest was served that night?"

Then he confronted in plain terms the contention that gay marriage would threaten the stability of heterosexual marriages. He said has never known a couple to divorce because two men lived next door—and certainly none of his Whitefish Bay neighbors had done so "because I love my partner." Nor will trashing homosexual unions strengthen heterosexual unions: "Indeed, if the sponsors of this amendment want to keep heterosexuals together then they should write an amendment banning divorce instead of one banning marriage."

Andrew closed with a reference to a member of his congregation who is an eighty-year-old Republican:

"I've been to his house. He's got a picture of President Bush on his kitchen counter. He signed a letter protesting this amendment because it is not just. He knew that baby Sienna, the youngest in our congregation, did not need politicians in Madison legislating against her family."

A month later, Andrew told his congregation of his legislative experience in a sermon entitled "Fragrant Faith" based on a reading from the Gospel of John. In it, he contrasted the hostility of the committee room with what he perceives as genuine Christian love. In Madison, he said, he caught "a glimpse of what it would be like to work for justice without devotion to Jesus; I don't think I could do it."

As he described his reception in Madison—"I can't think of another time I've been surrounded in a room with so much hatred, so many people convinced that my family is a threat to the fabric of society"—he choked up, unable for a few moments to continue. Later, he would be told that his profound emotion moved many in the congregation to their own tears.

He told them that when he returned to Milwaukee from Madison, he had come to the sanctuary to pray. "And I thought of my commitment ceremony here—the way so many of you supported me and Jay in making our covenant together and how many of you encouraged us in adopting our boys.

"I thanked God for the person who said, 'No matter what the legislature says, you're married in my eyes.'"

9.

The Outlook for Same-Sex Parenting: Overcoming the "Cheney Syndrome"

On the night of November 2, 2004, voters crammed into Portland Oregon's Melody Ballroom to celebrate the mayoral victory of Tom Potter, one of that election day's few wins by an outspoken proponent of gay marriage. (At a Portland City Club luncheon, for example, candidate Potter had publicly challenged Oregon's Democratic governor, the guest speaker, for his refusal to sanction the marriage of Potter's lesbian daughter.)

Now, shortly after Potter took the stage, arms raised in acknowledgment of the ear-splitting ovation, some 800 celebrants (their number limited by the size of the ball-room) were treated to a reprise of an interruption that had occurred nine months earlier when he was addressing a small gathering of supporters at a precam-paign meeting (see chapter 4): As the din calmed at Tom's urging, a tiny voice sang out from a few rows away, where five-year-old McKenzie Potter-Moen stood on a chair so she could see the stage. "Hi, Grandpa. Hi, Grandpa. Hi, Grandpa," she was shouting.

Tom glanced down at her, his smile broadened, and he called back, "Hi, Kenzie." Then he explained to the cel-ebrants, "That's my granddaughter McKenzie, and she likes to share the spotlight with her grandfather." His words drew another ovation, this time for Kenzie.

Eight months earlier Katie Potter and Pam Moen, the mothers of Kenzie and her little sister Madi, had capped their fifteen-year relationship with a wedding ceremony in Portland's Keller Auditorium (see chapter 4.) Now, their elation at Tom Potter's sweeping victory was mixed with sadness over other election results. The legality of their marriage seemed likely to have been undone by Oregon's adoption of a constitutional amendment banning gay marriage. Nationwide the same day, ten other states approved similar measures by resounding majorities ranging up to 86 percent in Mississippi. That brought to seventeen the number of states with such constitutional bans, and proponents immediately announced plans to introduce the bans in up to twenty more.

Indeed, in the weeks following the elections, many analysts credited George W. Bush's reelection as Presi-dent to a massive backlash triggered by the approval of gay marriage in Massachusetts a year earlier by the state's Supreme Court. The director of a conservative think tank quipped to the *Washington Post* that Bush should send a bouquet to Margaret Marshall, the Massachusetts chief justice, for doing "more than any other single person to assure his victory." Conservative Christian organizations immediately struck up a chorus of demands for a renewed push for a federal constitutional ban on gay marriage.

The Portland metropolitan area rejected the marriage ban by a whopping 62.5 to 37 percent. Statewide, however, 57 percent of the voters approved it—a substantial majority even if far less than in the other ten states adopting a ban that day. The precise extent of the damage to Katie's and Pam's legal rights would have to await the outcome of their litigation, as plaintiffs with eight other same-sex couples, on behalf of some three thousand similar pairs married the same month in two Oregon counties. (The marriages of two other couples whose stories are told here—those of Bonnie Tinker and Sara Graham [see chapter 1], and of Steven Lofton and Roger Croteau [see chapter 6]—likewise hinged on the same court action, the outcome of which was undecided at press time.)

⁓

In light of the devastating 2004 Election Day rejection of gay marriage throughout the country, how can I write, as I have in the introduction, that the opponents of same-sex unions "are fighting a doomed, rearguard action"?

Yes, the "Massachusetts backlash" perhaps—though not necessarily—slowed the progress toward equality. But I submit that the cultural power of the principal roadblock—something that might be termed the "Cheney Syndrome," discussed below—is irreversibly waning.

In the wake of the election, even many conservative Republicans openly expressed doubt as to the success of a proposed Federal constitutional ban on gay marriage. And even if such a measure were to succeed, it would likely soon end up in the same trash bin as the Eighteenth (Prohibition) Amendment, which was repealed little more than a decade after its adoption.

Meanwhile, even those antimarriage ballot measures tell only part of the 2004 Election Day story itself. In Ohio, where Bush's narrow edge tipped the national presidential scale and where 62 percent voted for the marriage ban, Cincinnati voters nonetheless repealed a ten-year-old antigay law barring legislation to protect gays and lesbians. In Missouri, where 71 percent had weeks earlier approved a marriage ban there, voters in November elected their first openly gay state legislator. Idaho and North Carolina did the same. In Portland, in addition to the mayoral election of outspoken gay marriage supporter Tom Potter, Sam Adams was elected Portland's first openly gay council member (see chapter 4). In Texas, arguably the nation's most conservative state, an openly lesbian woman won election as Dallas County sheriff. In Connecticut, openly gay legislator Art Feltman won 80 percent of the vote.

More directly to the point, Election Day exit polls

indicated that country-wide, about 60 percent of voters favored some sort of legal recognition for gay and lesbian couples. Nearly one third approved of full-scale marriage, and another third, while still unwilling to associate the word "marriage" with gay and lesbian partnerships, nevertheless indicated they favored civil unions that would confer many of the same legal rights. And those figures suggested that the favorable sentiment had perhaps actually increased since earlier in the year, when an ABC/*Washington Post* survey showed just a slight majority in favor of civil unions.

Those in favor of same-sex civil unions, moreover, include the man said to be the principal beneficiary of that "Massachusetts backlash," President George W. Bush himself. During the 2004 campaign, while maintaining his strong stance against gay marriage, Bush told an ABC interviewer, "I don't think we should deny people rights to a civil union, a legal arrangement, if that is what a state chooses to do." His words predictably drew immediate expressions of dismay from conservative religious groups and were squarely at odds with the Republican Party platform. The President nevertheless appeared to reinforce his stance during the third presidential debate. Asked whether he thought homosexuality was a choice, the President responded:

"I do know that we have a choice to make in America, and that is to treat people with tolerance and respect and dignity. . . . And I also know in a free society people, consenting adults, can live the way they want to live. And that's to be honored."

The future for same-sex unions is nowhere foretold

with more clarity than in the state of Vermont. There, in 1999, amid public uproar but by order of the state Supreme Court, the legislature legalized civil unions giving same-sex couples the same rights as married couples under state law. Signs demanding "Take Back Vermont" sprouted on roads throughout the state. In 2000, seventeen lawmakers who supported the law lost their bids for reelection, and Republicans gained control of the Vermont House. But in 2004 exit polls, only about one of five Vermont voters opposed both gay marriage and civil unions, and 40 percent said they favored full-scale marriage! Exposure to real human beings in caring, committed relationships had in just four years significantly eroded hateful, centuries-old stereotypes.

The same trend indisputably is occurring nationwide. When Vermont first legalized civil unions, in the words of National Public Radio's Bob Simon, "conservative political strategists reportedly rubbed their hands in happy anticipation of exploiting that issue in a political campaign." Now, just four years later, Simon pointedly observed, "permitting states to license civil unions has become the official policy of the newly reelected Republican president."

The extent of the President's expressed backing for fairness remains unclear. But the very fact that he would feel impelled to make the pronouncement he did, in defiance of his religious base at a critical juncture in a close election campaign, must necessarily have reflected a sharp turnabout by those "conservative political strategists." Opposition to civil unions, they must have concluded, was no longer politically viable.

Two other New England states, Connecticut and Massachusetts itself, reflected further evidence of the trend. Earlier in 2004, the Massachusetts legislature approved a constitutional amendment that would reverse the court's approval of gay marriage, if first passed again in the 2005 legislature and then approved by voters in November of 2006. On Election Day of 2004, however—after hundreds of lesbian and gay couples had actually been married there—every incumbent who opposed the amendment won reelection, while anti-amendment candidates were taking over six of eight open seats against pro-amendment candidates. Two pro-amendment incumbents were defeated, one by an openly gay candidate. By February of 2005, a Bay State Poll found an actual majority of state residents opposing the amendment. Bay State pollster Russell K. Mayer told the *Gloucester Daily Times* the result reflected a greater degree of acceptance of gay marriage: "We have it. The sky is not falling."

The Massachusetts events fall short of assuring ultimate defeat of the amendment. But as time passes, it would seem critical that those hundreds of same-sex marriages have apparently produced virtually no public controversy or uproar. Even the sponsor of the anti-marriage amendment conceded that the low-key manner of the gay weddings had eased the fears of many. So the Vermont experience is perhaps about to be repeated in Massachusetts.

In Connecticut, meanwhile, within a week after the election, the Republican governor and Republican House Minority Leader both conceded the likelihood that the legislature there would expand rights for same-sex couples. A Republican state senator said that the only issue was not whether rights would be granted, but how extensive they would be. (A perhaps bellwether election race saw the defeat of the most outspoken anti-gay-rights state senator, Win Smith, by a Democrat, Gayle Slossberg, who supports civil unions.)

In New York, the state attorney general ruled that even though same-sex marriages are prohibited by state law, the state nonetheless must recognize gay marriages and civil unions sanctioned in Vermont, Massachusetts, and Canada. New York City's Republican mayor followed up by ruling that such couples are entitled to the same city pension-fund rights as married heterosexual couples.

In general, the rights movement is certain to further accelerate as today's young people grow older, become a majority of our population, and spawn new national leaders with a fresh mindset. Polls of young people show rapidly increasing acceptance of lesbians and gay men. In the introduction, I write of the perhaps startling, but nonetheless highly prophetic, endorsement of gay marriage by the editors of the student newspaper at Baylor University, a Texas bastion of Christian Fundamentalism. In the days after the 2004 election, high school students walked out of class in such disparate locales as Eugene, Oregon, and Chicago, Illinois, to protest the gay marriage bans.

Evan Wolfson is the author of *Why Marriage Matters* and executive director of Freedom to Marry, a New York–based coalition. For his leadership in the campaign for gay marriage, *Time* magazine named him one of the

"100 Most Important People in the World Today." In the bluntest of terms, Wolfson says, "We have a secret weapon—death." By which, he explains, he means generational momentum: "Younger people overwhelmingly support ending this discrimination."

Pointing out that civil rights legislation came only after years of upheaval and backlash, Wolfson is confident that the movement toward gay marriage is on course, following what he calls "the classic American pattern of civil rights advance."

"It's patchwork," he explains. "Some states move toward equality faster, while others resist and even regress." But meanwhile, "Nothing is more transformative, nothing moves the middle more, than making it real, making it personal," as Middle America meets actual gay and lesbian couples.

So while the Massachusetts decision backlash has perhaps temporarily slowed the movement—even if not necessarily in Massachusetts itself—the end is clear. Many social scientists say the battle is actually over, and predict that same-sex marriage will gain majority support within the next generation or so.

Why, then, despite its ultimate inevitability, is acceptance of same-sex marriage so slow in coming? Conversely, why does acceptance indeed appear inevitable despite the fierceness of its opposition? And what fuels that fierceness to such heights as the powerful backlash to the Massachusetts court decision?

I suggest that the answer to all of these questions lies in what I have dubbed the "Cheney Syndrome."

A key development in the closing weeks of the 2004 presidential campaign was what the media commonly referred to as "the Mary Cheney flap." It was triggered in the final presidential debate when the candidates were asked by moderator Bob Schieffer whether homosexuality is a choice, and John Kerry responded:

"We're all God's children, Bob, and I think if you were to talk to Dick Cheney's daughter, who is a lesbian, she would tell you that she's being who she was. She's being who she was born as. I think if you talk to anybody, it's not a choice."

It was hardly the first time Mary Cheney's lesbianism had arisen in the campaign—or for that matter, in the last two presidential campaigns. In the 2000 vice-presidential debate—taking a more progressive stance than his Democratic debate opponent Joseph Lieberman—Cheney declined to rule out the propriety of gay marriage. "I think different states are likely to come to different conclusions and that's appropriate. I think we ought to do everything we can to tolerate and accommodate whatever kind of relationships people want to enter into." And in August of the 2004 campaign, he responded to a question about gay marriage by saying, "Lynne and I have a gay daughter, so it's an issue our family is very familiar with," adding that he personally disagrees with Bush's policy supporting a federal constitutional amendment banning gay marriage.

Mary Cheney herself has long been out as lesbian, served for years as Coors Brewing Company's liaison to the gay community, and regularly appeared on the campaign trail in the company of her partner Heather Poe.

Nevertheless, from the reaction to Kerry's reference to Mary Cheney, you'd have thought he had outed her. An *ABC News* poll found two out of three voters thought the remark "inappropriate." Seething, righteous columnists set off volleys of condemnation. Syndicated columnist Robert Novak called it an "insult." *New York Times* columnist William Safire called it a "low blow" bereft of any "sense of decency." Even the *Washington Post*'s pro-Kerry columnist Richard Cohen called Kerry a "political klutz" and "no gentleman." *Fox News* panelist Mort Kondrake called it "dirty pool." Dick Morris, a former strategist for Bill Clinton, called it a "horrible" and "vicious" tactic.

Strikingly under the circumstances, Dick and Lynne Cheney actually led the attack. Lynne Cheney, speaking as "an indignant mother," called Kerry "not a good man" and his comment a "cheap and tawdry political trick." Dick Cheney told supporters at a Florida rally, "You saw a man who will do and say anything to get elected," and described himself as "a pretty angry father."

In all the torrent of denunciation, however, there was no hint as to exactly *why*—in light of the reams of prior publicity about Mary Cheney's sexual orientation—Kerry's mention of it should be seen as insulting, indecent, or ungentlemanly. The *why*, apparently, was so obvious to most people that it required no explanation. But it's the key to popular resistance to gay marriage — the tacit cultural assumption that it's shameful to be gay.

If homosexuality is not shameful, on the other hand, the responses to Kerry's remark make no sense. An observation that one of Cheney's daughters was blond, or had children, or worked in his campaign, plainly would not have been seen by anyone as indecent, ungentlemanly, or tawdry.

To fully understand the underlying psychology, I refer you to a friend of mine I'll call "Jim."

Jim was one of the early white civil rights activists. Nearly half a century ago, he and his wife purchased a home in a planned integrated community composed of roughly half whites and half Negroes, as African Americans were then called. There, they raised three children, a boy and two girls, who grew up essentially indifferent to the skin color of their diverse neighborhood playmates.

So it should have come as no surprise, much less shock, when one of his daughters, Ann, started dating a black boy. But shocked—and heartily disapproving—Jim was. "My intellectual beliefs were out of sync with my guts," he says. "I, the great interracial pioneer of the integrated tract!" Then his second daughter, Beth, brought home her life partner—another woman—and Jim discovered another, deeper layer of prejudice. "I had raised hell about Ann having a black boyfriend," he says. "But boy, then I wished Beth had done the same thing."

Jim doesn't think homosexuality is "wrong," any more than he thinks racism is right, and he fully accepts and supports Beth and her life partner. Still, he says feelingly, "I wish with all my heart that Beth was straight."

Among parents who genuinely love their children—such

as the Cheneys—Jim's reaction is classic. But the clarity of Jim's insight into his ambivalence, the realization that his "beliefs and guts are out of sync," is perhaps unusual. Assuming, perhaps charitably, that the Cheneys reaction to the Kerry remark was genuine, their minds and guts, like Jim's were out of sync. And they went with their gut reaction without stopping to analyze the cruel message— "homosexuality is shameful"—that they were sending.

By conventional standards, if someone sees fit to refer to his own family's shame—a child's arrest for stealing or persistent drunk driving, say—that's one thing. But for someone else to bring it up publicly would be, yes, indecent, ungentlemanly, cheap, and tawdry. Hence, the response of all of those who condemned Kerry's remark becomes understandable when you realize that all of them—apparently including the vice president and his wife—were letting their conditioned prejudices rule their reason. This is what I have chosen to label the "Cheney Syndrome"—the condition where one's belief is out of sync with one's gut, and the gut rules.

In chapter 5, I quote a revealing excerpt from an essay by the daughter of lesbians who writes that for years she was baffled as to why she felt ashamed of her mothers even while firmly believing there is nothing wrong with same-sex love. Her words are worth repeating here:

"It took me a long time to realize what was right in front of my face, and an equally long time to accept it. The answer was that even though I truly believe that homosexuality was just as valid and natural as heterosexuality, I was living in a society that didn't. . . . Over the years, I had heard and seen enough to make me feel ashamed of my family, even though I knew there was nothing wrong with it."

Columnist Cohen—in general, a reliably gay-friendly columnist—unknowingly demonstrated the "Cheney Syndrome" when he wrote that while he "flinched" at Kerry's words, it was for reasons he found "hard to explain" in light of the earlier publicity about Mary Cheney's sexual orientation. Well, he probably "flinched" because his deeper feelings, despite his reasoned beliefs, told him that lesbianism is something that those outside the family simply don't mention.

Like so many in a homophobic culture, Cohen and the Cheneys apparently continue to feel—not necessarily *think*, but *feel*—that homosexuality is some sort of psychological and/or biological affliction, at root something shameful. Thus, as for most essentially gay-friendly Americans of older generations, their minds and guts are often, understandably, at odds. They grew up—as did I—in an era in which revulsion of homosexuality was an accepted, never-questioned aspect of the cultural climate, in a sense part of the very air we breathed.

The assumption that to be gay was to be sick or sinful, or both, was ingrained in our deepest feelings. As we met openly gay individuals we liked or admired, our minds gradually adjusted to the reality, and we began to realize that our feelings were in error. But the roots of the bias run deep and it perhaps never wholly disappears just because our minds tell us it's wrong. Our minds and our emotions often tell us conflicting stories—and civil rights progress always starts as a matter of mind over pernicious conditioning.

It's possible, of course, that the Cheneys' response was pure political calculation. (One report even had it that Mary Cheney herself suggested the attack mode.) If so—while cheap, indecent, and tawdry—it was indeed a shrewd move, capitalizing on the fact that voters as a whole perceive their daughter's lesbianism as shameful. (On the other hand, if the Cheneys' response was in fact spontaneous and genuine, I hope they subsequently had the decency to apologize to their daughter.)

Either way, the flap over the incident reveals both the depth of the residue of cultural homophobia and, at the same time, the inevitability of its surrender to ultimate acceptance of same-sex unions. Even if the Cheneys do in fact feel some residual sense of shame about a daughter's sexual orientation, it's clear that for the most part they are refusing to give it precedence over their sense of fairness. In the face of presumably heavy political pressure, they firmly and openly renounced the party line about a federal gay marriage amendment.

Their personal adjustment mirrors that of millions of parents of GLBT children (such as myself) who have learned, or are learning—whatever messages we might be receiving from our deep-rooted prejudice—that gay is not bad, it is simply different. Millions of others are going through the same process, by coming to know and like GLBT people at their jobs, churches, clubs, and other activities. Thousands of corporations have already learned that gay-friendly policies are good business: Nearly half of *Fortune* 500 companies offer domestic partner benefits, according to the Human Rights Campaign. And among those companies, 60 percent extend adoption assistance to the domestic partner, and 72 percent also allow employees to take extended family leave to care for a domestic partner or their dependents.

And, again, the importance of the generational gap in this regard cannot be overstated. With GLBT youth coming out at earlier and earlier ages, and gay- and lesbian-parented families becoming more and more visible, a large proportion of future generations will grow up without ever internalizing the kind of negative stereotypes that have plagued us older folk.

In the days after Election 2004, the *Pittsburgh Post-Gazette* summed up its reaction to the deluge of anti-gay-marriage ballot measures, in words that reflect both the slow pace and ultimate inevitably of national acceptance of families with same-sex parents:

"Despair is premature. . . . It may take some time, but such fundamental unfairness will one day be seen for what it is: immoral and un-American."

Appendix A

Policy Positions and Statements of Professional Organizations

As mentioned in the introduction, virtually every leading professional organization that deals with child welfare has issued statements supporting equal rights for same-sex parents and their children. Following are some examples:

American Anthropological Association

The following statement was released by the Executive Board, February 25, 2004, "in response to President Bush's call for a constitutional amendment banning gay marriage as a threat to civilization."

"The results of more than a century of anthropological research on households, kinship relationships, and families, across cultures and through time, provide no support whatsoever for the view that either civilization or viable social orders depend upon marriage as an exclusively heterosexual institution. Rather, anthropological research supports the conclusion that a vast array of family types, including families built upon same-sex partnerships, can contribute to stable and humane societies.

"The Executive Board of the American Anthropological Association strongly opposes a constitutional amendment limiting marriage to heterosexual couples."

North American Council on Adoptable Children

"Children should not be denied a permanent family because of the sexual orientation of potential parents. Everyone with the potential to successfully parent a child in foster care or adoption is entitled to fair and equal consideration."

—*Adopted March 14, 1998, as amended April 14, 2002*

American Academy of Pediatrics

"Children deserve to know that their relationships with both of their parents are stable and legally recognized. This applies to all children, whether their parents are of the same or opposite sex. The American Academy of Pediatrics recognizes that a considerable body of professional literature provides evidence that children with parents who are homosexual can have the same advantages and the same expectations for health, adjustment, and development as can children whose parents are heterosexual. When two adults participate in parenting a child, they and the child deserve the serenity that comes with legal recognition.

"Children born or adopted into families headed by partners who are of the same sex usually have only one biologic or adoptive legal parent. The other partner in a parental role is called the "co-parent" or "second parent." Because these families and children need the permanence and security that are provided by having two fully sanctioned and legally defined parents, the Academy supports the legal adoption of children by co-parents or second parents. Denying legal parent status through adoption to co-parents or second parents prevents these children from enjoying the psychologic and legal security that comes from having two willing, capable, and loving parents.

"Several states have considered or enacted legislation sanctioning second-parent adoption by partners of the same sex. In addition, legislative initiatives assuring legal status equivalent to marriage for gay and lesbian partners, such as the law approving civil unions in Vermont, can also attend to providing security and permanence for the children of those partnerships.

"Many states have not yet considered legislative actions to ensure the security of children whose parents are gay or lesbian. Rather, adoption has been decided by probate or family courts on a case-by-case basis. Case precedent is limited. It is important that a broad ethical mandate exist nationally that will guide the courts in providing necessary protection for children through co-parent adoption.

"Co-parent or second-parent adoption protects the child's right to maintain continuing relationships with both parents. The legal sanction provided by co-parent adoption accomplishes the following:

1. Guarantees that the second parent's custody rights and responsibilities will be protected if the first parent were to die or become incapacitated. Moreover, second-parent adoption protects the child's legal right of relationships with both parents. In the absence of co-parent adoption, members of the family of the legal parent, should he or she become incapacitated, might successfully challenge the surviving co-parent's rights to continue to parent the child, thus causing the child to lose both parents.

2. Protects the second parent's rights to custody and visitation if the couple separates. Likewise, the child's right to maintain relationships with both parents after separation, viewed as important to a positive outcome

in separation or divorce of heterosexual parents, would
be protected for families with gay or lesbian parents.

3. Establishes the requirement for child support from
both parents in the event of the parents' separation.

4. Ensures the child's eligibility for health benefits from
both parents.

5. Provides legal grounds for either parent to provide consent for medical care and to make education, health care,
and other important decisions on behalf of the child.

6. Creates the basis for financial security for children in
the event of the death of either parent by ensuring eligibility to all appropriate entitlements, such as Social
Security survivors benefits.

"On the basis of the acknowledged desirability that
children have and maintain a continuing relationship
with two loving and supportive parents, the Academy
recommends that pediatricians do the following:

• Be familiar with professional literature regarding gay
and lesbian parents and their children.

• Support the right of every child and family to the financial, psychologic, and legal security that results from
having legally recognized parents who are committed to
each other and to the welfare of their children.

• Advocate for initiatives that establish permanency through co-parent or second-parent adoption for children of same-sex partners through the judicial system, legislation, and community education.

—*Policy Statement of the Committee on Psychosocial Aspects of Child and Family Health, February 2002*

Child Welfare League of America

3.18 Nondiscrimination in selecting foster parents

The family foster care agency should not reject foster parent applicants solely due to their age, income, marital status, race, religious preference, sexual orientation, physical or disabling condition, or location of the foster home.

4.7 Nondiscrimination in provision of services to adoptive applicants.

All applicants should be assessed on the basis of their abilities to successfully parent a child needing family membership and not on their race, ethnicity or culture, income, age, marital status, religion, appearance, differing lifestyle, or sexual orientation.

Applicants should be accepted on the basis of an individual assessment of their capacity to understand and meet the needs of a particular available child at the point of the adoption and in the future.

—From CWLA Standards of Excellence for Adoption Services, 2000

American Psychoanalytic Association

"The American Psychoanalytic Association supports the position that the salient consideration in decisions about parenting, including conception, child rearing, adoption, visitation and custody is the best interest of the child. Accumulated evidence suggests the best interest of the child requires attachment to committed, nurturing and competent parents. Evaluation of an individual or couple for these parental qualities should be determined without prejudice regarding sexual orientation. Gay and lesbian individuals and couples are capable of meeting the best interest of the child and should be afforded the same rights and should accept the same responsibilities as heterosexual parents. With the adoption of this position statement, we support research studies that further our understanding of the impact of both traditional and gay/lesbian parenting on a child's development."

—Adopted May 2002

American Psychiatric Association (2002)

"Numerous studies over the last three decades consistently demonstrate that children raised by gay or lesbian parents exhibit the same level of emotional, cognitive, social, and sexual functioning as children raised by heterosexual parents. This research indicates that optimal development for children is based not on the sexual orientation of the parents, but on stable attachments to committed and nurturing adults. The research also shows that children who have two parents regardless of the parents' sexual orientations, do better than children with only one parent.

"While some states have approved legislation sanctioning second-parent adoption, other court judgments and legislation have prohibited lesbian women and gay men from adopting or co-parenting. Therefore, in most of the United States, only one partner in a committed gay or lesbian couple may have a legal parental relationship to a child they are raising together. Adoption by a second parent, however, would not only formalize a child's existing relationships with both parents in a same-sex couple, it would also provide vital security for the child. Children could avail themselves of both parents' health insurance benefits, access to medical care, death benefits, inheritance rights, and child support from both parents in the event of separation. Adoption protects both parents' rights to custody and/or visitation if the couple separates or if one parents dies.

"The American Psychiatric Association has historically supported equity, parity, and nondiscrimination regarding legal issues affecting mental health. In 2000, APA supported the legal recognition of same sex unions and their associated legal rights, benefits, and responsibilities. APA has also supported efforts to education the public about homosexuality and the mental health needs of lesbian women, gay men, and their families. Removing legal barriers that adversely affect the emotional and physical health of children raised by lesbian and gay parents is consistent with the goals of the APA.

"The American Psychiatric Association supports initiatives which allow same-sex couples to adopt and co-parent children and supports all the associated legal rights, benefits, and responsibilities which arise from such initiatives.

"This position statement was drafted and proposed by the Committee on Gay, Lesbian, and Bisexual Issues and was supported by the Council on Minority Mental Health and Health Disparities."

—*Approved by the Board of Trustees, November 2002*
—*Approved by the Assembly, November 2002*

American Psychiatric Association (2000)

"The American Psychiatric Association supports the legal recognition of same-sex unions and their associated legal rights, benefits and responsibilities.

"The APA expresses a valid interest in the well being of heterosexual married couples in such areas as children's mental health and other aspects of family life. Heterosexual relationships have a legal framework for their existence, which provides a stabilizing force.

"In the United States, with the recent exception of Vermont, same-sex partners are currently denied the important benefits and responsibilities of legal marriage. Same-sex couples therefore experience several kinds of state-sanctioned discrimination that affect the stability of their relationships.

"The children of gay and lesbian parents do not have the same protection that legal marriage affords the children of heterosexual couples. Adoptive and divorced lesbian and gay parents face additional obstacles. An adoptive parent who is lesbian or gay is presumed unfit in many U.S. jurisdictions. Furthermore, when couples do adopt, usually one parent is granted legal rights, while the other parent may have no legal standing. These obstacles occur even though research has shown that the children raised by lesbian and gay men are as well adjusted as those reared within heterosexual relationships.

"The American Psychiatric Association has historically supported equity, parity, and nondiscrimination regarding legal issues affecting mental health. Educating the public about lesbian and gay relationships and supporting efforts to establish same-sex legal unions is consistent with the Association's advocacy for other disadvantaged minority group."

> —*Approved by the Board of Trustees, December 2000*
> —*Approved by the Assembly, November 2000*

American Psychological Association

"WHEREAS APA has a long-established policy to deplore 'all public and private discrimination against gay men and lesbians' and urges 'the repeal of all discriminatory legislation against lesbians and gay men' . . . ;

"WHEREAS the APA adopted the Resolution on Legal Benefits for Same-Sex Couples in 1998 . . . ;

"WHEREAS Discrimination and prejudice based on sexual orientation detrimentally affects psychological, physical, social, and economic well-being . . . ;

"WHEREAS "Anthropological research on households, kinship relationships, and families, across cultures and through time, provide[s] no support whatsoever for the view that either civilization or viable social orders depend upon marriage as an exclusively heterosexual institution." (American Anthropological Association, 2004);

"WHEREAS Psychological research on relationships and couples provides no evidence to justify discrimination against same-sex couples . . . ;

"WHEREAS The institution of civil marriage confers a social status and important legal benefits, rights and privileges;

"WHEREAS The United States General Accounting Office (2004) has identified over 1,000 federal statutory provisions in which marital status is a factor in determining or receiving benefits, rights, and privileges, for example, those concerning taxation, federal loans, and dependent and survivor benefits (e.g., Social Security, military, and veterans);

"WHEREAS There are numerous state, local, and private sector laws and other provisions in which marital status is a factor in determining or receiving benefits, rights, and privileges, for example, those concerning taxation, health insurance, health care decision-making, property rights, pension and retirement benefits, and inheritance;

"WHEREAS Same-sex couples are denied equal access to civil marriage;

"WHEREAS Same-sex couples who enter into a civil union are denied equal access to all the benefits, rights, and privileges provided by federal law to married couples (United States General Accounting Office, 2004);

"WHEREAS The benefits, rights, and privileges associated with domestic partnerships are not universally available, and are not equal to those associated with marriage, and are rarely portable;

"WHEREAS people who also experience discrimination based on age, race, ethnicity, disability, gender and gender identity, religion, and socioeconomic status may especially benefit from access to marriage to same-sex couples . . . ;

"THEREFORE BE IT RESOLVED That the APA believes that it is unfair and discriminatory to deny same-sex couples legal access to civil marriage and to all its attendant benefits, rights, and privileges;

"THEREFORE BE IT FURTHER RESOLVED That APA shall take a leadership role in opposing all discrimination in legal benefits, rights, and privileges against same-sex couples;

"THEREFORE BE IT FURTHER RESOLVED That APA encourages psychologists to act to eliminate all discrimination against same-sex couples in their practice, research, education and training . . . ;

"THEREFORE BE IT FURTHER RESOLVED That the APA shall provide scientific and educational resources that inform public discussion and public policy development regarding sexual orientation and marriage and that assist its members, divisions, and affiliated state, provincial, and territorial psychological associations."

—*Adopted by the American Psychological Association Council of Representatives, July 2004.*

— *Note: The original Resolution contains extensive supporting citations and references that have been omitted here.*

National Association of Social Workers

"Social workers are guided by the NASW Code of Ethics (1996), which bans the discrimination on the basis of sexual orientation and encourages social workers to act to expand access, choices, and opportunities for oppressed people and groups. It is the policy of NASW that same-gender sexual orientation should be afforded the same respect and rights as other-gender orientation. Discrimination and prejudice directed against any group are damaging to the social, emotional, and economic well-being of the affected group and of society as a whole. NASW is committed to advancing the policies and practices that will improve the status of all lesbian, gay, bisexual, and transgender people.

"NASW works in coalition with mental health and other human services professions to help enact antidiscrimination legislation at national, state, and local levels and actively campaigns against any laws allowing anti-discriminatory practices against lesbian, gay, bisexual, and transgender people, primarily in immigration, employment, housing, professional credentialing, licensing, public accommodation, child custody, and the right to marry. (NASW, 1996)."

—*From "Social Work Speaks," 6th edition, NASW Policy Statements, 2003–2006.*

American Academy of Child & Adolescent Psychiatry

"The basis on which all decisions relating to custody and parental rights should rest on the best interest of the child. Lesbian, gay, and bisexual individuals historically have faced more rigorous scrutiny than heterosexuals regarding their rights to be or become parents.

"There is no evidence to suggest or support that parents with a gay, lesbian, or bisexual orientation are per se different from or deficient in parenting skills, child-centered concerns and parent-child attachments, when compared to parents with a heterosexual orientation. It has long been established that a homosexual orientation is not related to psychopathology, and there is no basis on which to assume that a parental homosexual orientation will increase likelihood of or induce a homosexual orientation in the child.

"Outcome studies of children raised by parents with a homosexual or bisexual orientation, when compared to heterosexual parents, show no greater degree of instability in the parental relationship or developmental dysfunction in children.

"The AACAP opposes any discrimination based on sexual orientation against individuals in regard to their rights as custodial or adoptive parents as adopted by Council."

—Approved by Council, June, 1999

American Medical Association

Our AMA will support legislative and other efforts to allow the adoption of a child by the same-sex partner, or opposite sex nonmarried partner, who functions as a second parent or co-parent to that child.

> —*Policy adopted by the AMA, June 2004, on the basis
> of the following resolution submitted by its Medical
> Student Section:*

WHEREAS, Having two fully sanctioned and legally defined parents promotes a safe and nurturing environment for children, including psychological and legal security; and

WHEREAS, Children born or adopted into families headed by partners who are of the same sex usually have only one biologic or adoptive legal parent; and

WHEREAS, The legislative protection afforded to children of parents in homosexual relationships varies from state to state, with some states enacting or considering legislation sanctioning co-parent or second parent adoption by partners of the same sex, several states declining to consider legislation, and at least one state altogether banning adoption by the second parent; and

WHEREAS, Co-parent or second parent adoption guarantees that the second parent's custody rights and responsibilities are protected if the first parent dies or becomes incapacitated; and

WHEREAS, Co-parent or second parent adoption ensures the child's eligibility for health benefits from both parents and establishes the requirement for child support from both parents in the event of the parents' separation; and

WHEREAS, Co-parent or second parent adoption establishes legal grounds to provide consent for medical care and to make health care decisions on behalf of the child and guarantees visitation rights if the child becomes hospitalized; and

WHEREAS, The American Academy of Pediatrics and the American Psychiatric Association have each issued statements supporting initiatives which allow same-sex couples to adopt and co-parent children; therefore be it

RESOLVED, That our American Medical Association support legislative and other efforts to allow the adoption of a child by the same-sex partner, or opposite sex nonmarried partner, who functions as a second parent or co-parent to that child. (New HOD Policy)

Appendix B

A Conversation with Professor Judith Stacey

*Reprinted with permission from "Too High A Price:
The Case Against Restricting Gay Parenting,"
American Civil Liberties Union, 2002. (Dr. Stacey's
answers were reviewed and updated by her in 2004.)*

Judith Stacey is a senior scholar with the Council on Contemporary Families and Professor of Sociology at New York University. In 2001, she and Timothy J. Biblarz published a review of the social science research on lesbian and gay parenting called, "(How) Does the Sexual Orientation of Parents Matter?" in the *American Sociological Review*.

Florida and conservative activists everywhere argue that heterosexuals make better parents than gay men or lesbians. Is there anything in the body of social science research that supports this claim?

No, nothing at all. Significant, reliable social scientific evidence indicates that lesbian and gay parents are as fit, effective and successful as heterosexual parents. The research also shows that children of same-sex couples are as emotionally healthy and socially adjusted and at least as educationally and socially successful as children raised by heterosexual parents. No credible social science evidence supports Florida's claim.

Florida and other states have used so-called experts in social science who try to discredit the studies you cite. They claim that these studies used flawed research methods and resulted in flawed findings. What is your response?

The studies that have been conducted are certainly not perfect—virtually no study is. It's almost never possible to transform complex social relationships, such as parent-child relationships, into adequate, quantifiable measures, and because many lesbians and gay men remain in the closet, we cannot know if the participants in the studies are representative of all gay people. However, the studies we reviewed are just as reliable and respected as studies in other areas of child development and psychology. So, most of those so-called experts are really leveling attacks on well-accepted social science methods. Yet they do not raise objections to studies that are even less rigorous or generalizable on such issues as the impact of divorce on children. It seems evident that the critics employ a double standard. They attack these particular studies not because the research methods differ from or are inferior to most studies of family relationships but because these critics do not like the findings.

The studies we discussed have been published in rigorously peer-reviewed and highly selective journals, whose standards represent expert consensus on generally accepted social scientific standards for research on child development. Those journals include *Child Development* and *Developmental Psychology*, the two flagship journals in the field of child development. The first is published by the five-thousand-member academic Society for Research in Child Development, and the second is published by the American Psychological Association.

There are other reviews and research out there that not only criticize the studies you cite but also come up with findings that actually say lesbians and gay men should not be parents. Why don't you include those studies in your review?

There is not a single, respectable social scientist conducting and publishing research in this area today who claims that gay and lesbian parents harm children. The dubious studies you mention were produced primarily by people who have been discredited and even expelled from the American Psychological Association (APA) and the American Sociological Association (ASA). When people claim that studies show gay parents harm children, they often cite people like Paul Cameron. Paul Cameron is the primary disreputable and discredited figure in this literature. He was expelled from the APA and censored by the ASA for unethical scholarly practices, such as selective, misleading representations of research and making claims that could not be substantiated.

In 2001, you and your colleague Tim Biblarz released a

new review of the existing studies on lesbian and gay parenting. This review caused a bit of a commotion in the media. Are people representing the review accurately? What did you say in the review that caused so much controversy?

In our review we found that many researchers in this field shied away from studying or analyzing any areas of difference between families with lesbian and gay parents and those with heterosexual parents. In contrast, we emphasized some of the scattered findings of small, but interesting differences that have been reported in some of this research. Conservative activists and journalists immediately seized on our discussion of these differences and began to cite these and our article as evidence in support of their efforts to deny partnership and parenting rights to lesbians and gay men. This is a serious misreading and abuse of our work. None of the significant differences reported in the research apply to child self-esteem, psychological well-being, or social adjustment. Nor were there differences in parents' self-esteem, mental health, or commitment to their children. In other words, even though we noted some differences, we emphasized that the differences were not deficits. In fact, the studies found no negative effects of lesbian and gay parenting, and a few studies reported some differences that could represent a few advantages of lesbian parenting.

What are some of the differences you observed?

Well, for example, several studies found that lesbian co-mothers share family responsibilities more equally than heterosexual married parents, and some research hints that children benefit from egalitarian co-parenting. A few studies found that lesbians worry less than heterosexual parents about the gender conformity of their children. Perhaps that helps to account for a few studies that found that sons of lesbians play less aggressively and that children of lesbians communicate their feelings more freely, aspire to a wider range of occupations, and score higher on self-esteem. I think most people would see these as positive things, but some of the critics have misrepresented these differences as evidence that the children are suffering from gender confusion. Finally, some studies reported that lesbian mothers feel more comfortable discussing sexuality with their children and accepting their children's sexuality—whatever it might be. More to the point are data reported in a twenty-five year British study. Although few of the young adults identified themselves as gay or lesbian, a larger minority of those with lesbian mothers did report that they had at one time or another considered or actually had a same-sex relationship.

Are you saying that the social science finds that children of lesbians and gays are more likely to be gay themselves?

Sexuality is far more complicated than that. Most gay adults, after all, were brought up by straight parents. We are still in the dark ages when it comes to understanding the roots of specific sexual attractions. Regardless of the relative impact of nature and nurture, it seems likely that growing up with gay parents should reduce a child's reluctance to acknowledge, accept, or act upon same-sex sexual desires if they experience them. Because the first generation of children parented by self-identified lesbians or gay men is only now reaching adulthood, it is too soon to know if the finding in that one study will prove to be generally true.

What are the factors in parents that have been shown to negatively impact children?

Some characteristics and circumstances of parents have been found consistently to correlate to problems in child development. These include: poverty, a low level of parental education, a high level of conflict between parents, and depression in parents.

Do you know of any studies currently underway that may shed more light on lesbian and gay parenting?

A new generation of research is continuing on donor-inseminated mothers and on gay custodial fathers, particularly on gay men who become fathers through surrogacy. Studies of lesbian parenthood in a growing number of nations are beginning to be publkished, and there is current research underway on lesbian mothers of color in the United States. There are also additional longitudinal studies of lesbian motherhood in progress in the United States and Europe.

What are the areas of gay parenting that you think new studies should explore?

There's a real need for a study on adoptive parents, one that compares children adopted by gay parents with children adopted by heterosexual parents. To my knowledge, there has never been such a study. We also need more research on gay fathers—especially studies that compare gay fathers to heterosexual fathers and studies that include gay fathers who have children through surrogacy or other means. And it's critical to expand studies with more diverse representations of lesbian and gay parents, specifically in terms of race, ethnicity, education, income, and nationality. Finally, the advent of legal same-sex marriage in Massachusetts, Canada, the Netherlands, and elsewhere provides an opportunity to compare married and unmarried parenting among same-sex as well as heterosexual couples.

Appendix C

10 facts

1. Same-sex couples live in 99.3 percent of all counties nationwide.

2. There are an estimated 3.1 million people living together in same-sex relationships in the United States.

3. Fifteen percent of these same-sex couples live in rural settings.

4. One out of three lesbian couples is raising children. One out of five gay male couples is raising children.

5. Between 1 million and 9 million children are being raised by gay, lesbian and bisexual parents in the United States today.

6. At least one same-sex couple is raising children in 96 percent of all counties nationwide.

7. The highest percentages of same-sex couples raising children live in the South.

8. Nearly one in four same-sex couples includes a partner 55 years old or older, and nearly one in five same-sex couples is composed of two people 55 or older.

9. More than one in 10 same-sex couples include a partner 65 years old or older, and nearly one in 10 same-sex couples is composed of two people 65 or older.

10. The states with the highest numbers of same-sex senior couples are also the most popular for heterosexual senior couples: California, New York and Florida.

These facts are based on analyses of the 2000 Census conducted by the Urban Institute and the Human Rights Campaign. The estimated number of people in same-sex relationships has been adjusted by 62 percent to compensate for the widely-reported undercount in the Census. (See "Gay and Lesbian Families in the United States: Same-Sex Unmarried Partner Households" on *www.hrc.org*.)

Why same-sex couples want to marry.

Many same-sex couples want the right to legally marry because they are in love — either they just met the love of their lives, or more likely, they have spent the last 10, 20 or 50 years with that person — and they want to honor their relationship in the greatest way our society has to offer, by making a public commitment to stand together in good times and bad, through all the joys and challenges family life brings.

Many parents want the right to marry because they know it offers children a vital safety net and guarantees protections that unmarried parents cannot provide.

And still other people — both gay and straight — are fighting for the right of same-sex couples to marry because they recognize that it is simply not fair to deny some families the protections all other families are eligible to enjoy.

Currently in the United States, same-sex couples in long-term, committed relationships pay higher taxes and are denied basic protections and rights granted to married heterosexual couples. Among them:

>> **Hospital visitation.** Married couples have the automatic right to visit each other in the hospital and make medical decisions. Same-sex couples can be denied the right to visit a sick or injured loved one in the hospital.

>> **Social Security benefits.** Married people receive Social Security payments upon the death of a spouse. Despite paying payroll taxes, gay and lesbian partners receive no Social Security survivor benefits — resulting in an average annual income loss of $5,528 upon the death of a partner.

>> **Immigration.** Americans in binational relationships are not permitted to petition for their same-sex partners to immigrate. As a result, they are often forced to separate or move to another country.

>> Health insurance. Many public and private employers provide medical coverage to the spouses of their employees, but most employers do not provide coverage to the life partners of gay and lesbian employees. Gay employees who do receive health coverage for their partners must pay federal income taxes on the value of the insurance.

>> Estate taxes. A married person automatically inherits all the property of his or her deceased spouse without paying estate taxes. A gay or lesbian taxpayer is forced to pay estate taxes on property inherited from a deceased partner.

>> Retirement savings. While a married person can roll a deceased spouse's 401(k) funds into an IRA without paying taxes, a gay or lesbian American who inherits a 401(k) can end up paying up to 70 percent of it in taxes and penalties.

>> Family leave. Married workers are legally entitled to unpaid leave from their jobs to care for an ill spouse. Gay and lesbian workers are not entitled to family leave to care for their partners.

>> Nursing homes. Married couples have a legal right to live together in nursing homes. Because they are not legal spouses, elderly gay or lesbian couples do not have the right to spend their last days living together in nursing homes.

>> Home protection. Laws protect married seniors from being forced to sell their homes to pay high nursing home bills; gay and lesbian seniors have no such protection.

>> Pensions. After the death of a worker, most pension plans pay survivor benefits only to a legal spouse of the participant. Gay and lesbian partners are excluded from such pension benefits.

Why civil unions aren't enough.

Comparing marriage to civil unions is a bit like comparing diamonds to rhine-stones. One is, quite simply, the real deal; the other is not. Consider:

>> Couples eligible to marry may have their marriage performed in any state and have it recognized in every other state in the nation and every country in the world.

>> Couples who are joined in a civil union in Vermont (the only state that offers civil unions) have no guarantee that its protections will even travel with them to neighboring New York or New Hampshire — let alone California or any other state.

Moreover, even couples who have a civil union and remain in Vermont receive only second-class protections in comparison to their married friends and neighbors. While they receive state-level protections, they do not receive any of the *more than 1,100 federal benefits and protections of marriage.*

In short, civil unions are not separate but equal — they are separate *and* unequal. And our society has tried separate before. It just doesn't work.

Marriage:	Civil unions:
• State grants marriage licenses to couples.	• State would grant civil union licenses to couples.
• Couples receive legal protections and rights under state and federal law.	• Couples receive legal protections and rights under state law only.
• Couples are recognized as being married by the federal government and all state governments.	• Civil unions are not recognized by other states or the federal government.
• Religious institutions are not required to perform marriage ceremonies.	• Religious institutions are not required to perform civil union ceremonies.

Answers to Questions

People are Asking

"I believe God meant marriage for men and women. How can I support marriage for same-sex couples?"

Many people who believe in God — and fairness and justice for all — ask this question. They feel a tension between religious beliefs and democratic values that has been experienced in many different ways throughout our nation's history. That is why the framers of our Constitution established the principle of separation of church and state. That principle applies no less to the marriage issue than it does to any other.

Indeed, the answer to the apparent dilemma between religious beliefs and support for equal protections for all families lies in recognizing that marriage has a significant religious meaning for many people, but that it is also a legal contract. And it is strictly the legal — not the religious — dimension of marriage that is being debated now.

Granting marriage rights to same-sex couples would *not* require Christianity, Judaism, Islam or any other religion to perform these marriages. It would not require religious institutions to permit these ceremonies to be held on their grounds. It would not even require that religious communities discuss the issue. People of faith would remain free to make their own judgments about what makes a marriage in the eyes of God — just as they are today.

Consider, for example, the difference in how the Catholic Church and the U.S. government view couples who have divorced and remarried. Because church tenets do not sanction divorce, the second marriage is not valid in the church's view. The government, however, recognizes the marriage by extending to the remarried couple the same rights and protections as those granted to every other married couple in America. In this situation — as would be the case in marriage for same-sex couples — the church remains free to establish its own teachings on the religious dimension of marriage while the government upholds equality under law.

It should also be noted that there are a growing number of religious communities that have decided to bless same-sex unions. Among them are Reform Judaism, the Unitarian Universalist Association and the Metropolitan Community Church. The Presbyterian Church (USA) also allows ceremonies to be performed, although they are not considered the same as marriage. The Episcopal Church and United Church of Christ allow individual churches to set their own policies on same-sex unions.

"This is different from interracial marriage. Sexual orientation is a choice."

"We cannot keep turning our backs on gay and lesbian Americans. I have fought too hard and too long against discrimination based on race and color not to stand up against discrimination based on sexual orientation. I've heard the reasons for opposing civil marriage for same-sex couples. Cut through the distractions, and they stink of the same fear, hatred, and intolerance I have known in racism and in bigotry."

— *Rep. John Lewis, D-Ga., a leader of the black civil rights movement, writing in* The Boston Globe, *Nov. 25, 2003*

Decades of research all point to the fact that sexual orientation is not a choice, and that a person's sexual orientation cannot be changed. Who one is drawn to is a fundamental aspect of who we are.

In this way, the struggle for marriage equality for same-sex couples is just as basic as the fight for interracial marriage was. It recognizes that Americans should not be coerced into false and unhappy marriages but should be free to marry the person they love — thereby building marriage on a true and stable foundation.

"Won't this create a free-for-all and make the whole idea of marriage meaningless?"

Many people share this concern because opponents of gay and lesbian people have used this argument as a scare tactic. But it is not true. Granting same-sex couples the right to marry would in no way change the number of people who could enter into a marriage (or eliminate restrictions on the age or familial relationships of those who may marry). Marriage would continue to recognize the highest possible commitment that can be made between two adults, plain and simple.

Organizations that Support Same-sex Parenting:

American Academy of Pediatrics
American Academy of Family Physicians
Child Welfare League of America
National Association of Social Workers
North American Council on Adoptable Children
American Bar Association
American Psychological Association
American Psychiatric Association
American Psychoanalytic Association

"I strongly believe children need a mother and a father."

Many of us grew up believing that everyone needs a mother and father, regardless of whether we ourselves happened to have two parents, or two *good* parents.

But as families have grown more diverse in recent decades, and researchers have studied how these different family relationships affect children, it has become clear that the *quality* of a family's relationship is more important than the particular *structure* of families that exist today. In other words, the qualities that help children grow into good and responsible adults — learning how to learn, to have compassion for others, to contribute to society and be respectful of others and their differences — do not depend on the sexual orientation of their parents but on their parents' ability to provide a loving, stable and happy home, something no class of Americans has an exclusive hold on.

That is why research studies have consistently shown that children raised by gay and lesbian parents do just as well on all conventional measures of child development, such as academic achievement, psychological well-being and social abilities, as children raised by heterosexual parents.

That is also why the nation's leading child welfare organizations, including the American Academy of Pediatrics, the American Academy of Family Physicians and others, have issued statements that dismiss assertions that only heterosexual couples can be good parents — and declare that the focus should now be on providing greater protections for the 1 million to 9 million children being raised by gay and lesbian parents in the United States today.

"What would be wrong with a constitutional amendment to define marriage as a union of a man and woman?"

In more than 200 years of American history, the U.S. Constitution has been amended only 17 times since the Bill of Rights — and in each instance (except for Prohibition, which was repealed), it was to extend rights and liberties to the American people, not restrict them. For example, our Constitution was amended to end our nation's tragic history of slavery. It was also amended to guarantee people of color, young people and women the right to vote.

The amendment currently under consideration (called the Federal Marriage Amendment) would be the only one that would single out one class of Americans for discrimination by ensuring that same-sex couples would not be granted the equal protections that marriage brings to American families.

Moreover, the amendment could go even further by stripping same-sex couples of some of the more limited protections they now have, such as access to health insurance for domestic partners and their children.

Neither enshrining discrimination in our Constitution nor stripping millions of families of basic protections would serve our nation's best interest. The Constitution is supposed to protect and ensure equal treatment for *all* people. It should not be used to single out a group of people for different treatment.

Text of Proposed Federal Marriage Amendment:

"Marriage in the United States shall consist only of the union of a man and a woman.

Neither this [C]onstitution [n]or the constitution of any state, nor state or federal law, shall be construed to require that marital status or the legal incidents thereof be conferred upon unmarried couples or groups."

— H.J. Resolution 56, introduced by Rep. Marilyn Musgrave, R-Colo., in May 2003. It has more than 100 co-sponsors. A similar bill was introduced in the U.S. Senate in November 2003. In February 2004, President Bush said that he would support a constitutional amendment to define marriage as between only a man and a woman.

Appendix C

"How could marriage for same-sex couples possibly be good for the American family — or our country?"

> *"We shouldn't just allow gay marriage. We should insist on gay marriage. We should regard it as scandalous that two people could claim to love each other and not want to sanctify their love with marriage and fidelity."*
>
> — *Conservative Columnist David Brooks,*
> *writing in* The New York Times,
> *Nov. 22, 2003.*

The prospect of a significant change in our laws and customs has often caused people to worry more about dire consequences that could result than about the potential positive outcomes. In fact, precisely the same anxiety arose when some people fought to overturn the laws prohibiting marriage between people of different races in the 1950s and 1960s. (One Virginia judge even declared that "God intended to separate the races.")

But in reality, opening marriage to couples who are so willing to fight for it could only strengthen the institution for all. It would open the doors to more supporters, not opponents. And it would help keep the age-old institution alive.

As history has repeatedly proven, institutions that fail to take account of the changing needs of the population are those that grow weak; those that recognize and accommodate changing needs grow strong. For example, the U.S. military, like American colleges and universities, grew stronger after permitting African Americans and women to join its ranks.

Similarly, granting same-sex couples the right to marry would strengthen the institution of marriage by allowing it to better meet the needs of the true diversity of family structures in America today.

When gay or lesbian people grow old
and in need of nursing home care, there
is no legal document that can give them
the right to Medicaid coverage without
potentially causing their partner to be
forced from their home.

"Can't same-sex couples go to a lawyer to secure all the rights they need?"

Not by a long shot. When a gay or lesbian person gets seriously ill, there is no legal document that can make their partner eligible to take leave from work under the federal Family and Medical Leave Act to provide care — because that law applies only to married couples.

When gay or lesbian people grow old and in need of nursing home care, there is no legal document that can give them the right to Medicaid coverage without potentially causing their partner to be forced from their home — because the federal Medicaid law only permits married spouses to keep their home without becoming ineligible for benefits.

And when a gay or lesbian person dies, there is no legal document that can extend Social Security survivor benefits or the right to inherit a retirement plan without severe tax burdens that stem from being "unmarried" in the eyes of the law.

These are only a few examples of the critical protections that are granted through more than 1,100 federal laws that protect only married couples. In the absence of the right to marry, same-sex couples can only put in place a handful of the most basic arrangements, such as naming each other in a will or a power of attorney. And even these documents remain vulnerable to challenges in court by disgruntled family members.

"Won't this cost taxpayers too much money?"

No, it wouldn't necessarily cost much at all. In fact, treating same-sex couples as families under law could even save taxpayers money because marriage would require them to assume legal responsibility for their joint living expenses and reduce their dependence on public assistance programs, such as Medicaid, Temporary Assistance to Needy Families, Supplemental Security Income disability payments and food stamps.

Put another way, the money it would cost to extend benefits to same-sex couples could be outweighed by the money that would be saved as these families rely more fully on each other instead of state or federal government assistance.

For example, two studies conducted in 2003 by professors at the University of Massachusetts, Amherst, and the University of California, Los Angeles, found that extending domestic partner benefits to same-sex couples in California and New Jersey would save taxpayers millions of dollars a year.

Specifically, the studies projected that the California state budget would save an estimated $8.1 million to $10.6 million each year by enacting the most comprehensive domestic partner law in the nation. In New Jersey, which passed a new domestic partner law in 2004, the savings were projected to be even higher — more than $61 million each year.

(Sources: "Equal Rights, Fiscal Responsibility: The Impact of A.B. 205 on California's Budget," by M. V. Lee Badgett, Ph.D., IGLSS, Department of Economics, University of Massachusetts, and R. Bradley Sears, J.D., Williams Project, UCLA School of Law, University of California, Los Angeles, May 2003, and "Supporting Families, Saving Funds: A Fiscal Analysis of New Jersey's Domestic Partnership Act," by Badgett and Sears with Suzanne Goldberg, J.D., Rutgers School of Law-Newark, December 2003.)

"Where can same-sex couples marry today?"

In 2001, the Netherlands became the first country to extend marriage rights to same-sex couples. Belgium passed a similar law two years later. The laws in both of these countries, however, have strict citizenship or residency requirements that do not permit American couples to take advantage of the protections provided.

In June 2003, Ontario became the first Canadian province to grant marriage to same-sex couples, and in July 2003, British Columbia followed suit — becoming the first places that American same-sex couples could go to get married.

In November 2003, the Massachusetts Supreme Judicial Court recognized the right of same-sex couples to marry — giving the state six months to begin issuing marriage licenses to same-sex couples. It began issuing licenses May 17, 2004.

In February 2004, the city of San Francisco began issuing marriage licenses to same-sex couples after the mayor declared that the state constitution forbade him to discriminate. The issue is being addressed by California courts, and a number of other cities have either taken or are considering taking steps in the same direction.

Follow the latest developments in California, Oregon, New Jersey, New Mexico, New York and in other communities across the country on the HRC Marriage Center (*www.hrc.org/marriage*).

Other nations have also taken steps toward extending equal protections to all couples, though the protections they provide are more limited than marriage. Canada, Denmark, Finland, France, Germany, Iceland, Norway, Portugal and Sweden all have nationwide laws that grant same-sex partners a range of important rights, protections and obligations.

For example, in France, registered same-sex (and opposite-sex) couples can be joined in a civil "solidarity pact" that grants them the right to file joint tax returns, extend social security coverage to each other and receive the same health, employment and welfare benefits as legal spouses. It also commits the couple to assume joint responsibility for household debts.

Other countries, including Switzerland, Scotland and the Czech Republic, also have considered legislation that would legally recognize same-sex unions.

"What protections other than marriage are available to same-sex couples?"

At the federal level, there are no protections at all available to same-sex couples. In fact, a federal law called the "Defense of Marriage Act" says that the federal government will discriminate against same-sex couples who marry by refusing to recognize their marriages or providing them with the federal protections of marriage. Some members of Congress are trying to go even further by attempting to pass a Federal Marriage Amendment that would write discrimination against same-sex couples into the U.S. Constitution.

At the state level, only Vermont offers civil unions, which provide important state benefits but no federal protections, such as Social Security survivor benefits. There is also no guarantee that civil unions will be recognized outside Vermont. Thirty-nine states also have "defense of marriage" laws explicitly prohibiting the recognition of marriages between same-sex partners.

Domestic partner laws have been enacted in California, Connecticut, New Jersey, Hawaii and the District of Columbia. The benefits conferred by these laws vary; some offer access to family health insurance, others confer co-parenting rights. These benefits are limited to residents of the state. A family that moves out of these states immediately loses the protections.

Reprinted with permission from "Answers to Questions About Marriage Equality," a brochure produced by the Human Rights Campaign Foundation. Visit www.hrc.org for more information.

Acknowledgments

Plainly, I could not have undertaken this book without the wholehearted cooperation of the families I have sketched. Their willingness to go public with their stories reflects not only their personal courage, but their faith in a better and fairer America. I am deeply grateful to all of them.

My daughters, Sharon and Bobbi, and my son-in-law John Sheehan, gave generously of their time and editorial acumen to review early drafts and offer thoughtful critiques and suggestions, many of which have informed the book's eventual shape and substance. Nor could I have completed it without the patience and cooperation of my wife, Myrna, who as always graciously put up with my often selfish preoccupation with my project; whose caring presence at many of the interviews helped create an atmosphere of warmth and acceptance that encouraged the subjects to open their lives to us; and who reviewed and critiqued a manuscript draft.

I am as always indebted to my agent Frances Goldin and her superlative, insightful colleague Sydelle Kramer. The attentive cooperation of Matthew Lore, Vice President and Publisher of Marlowe & Company, has been invaluable. I am also indebted to Marlowe's Peter Jacoby for computer-age guidance to a tech-impaired author.

Thanks also the public information personnel at various professional organizations, most notably Paul Cates of the American Civil Liberties Union, for his unfailingly efficient response to my many queries regarding *Lofton v. Kramer* and the informative ACLU booklet, "Too High A Price."